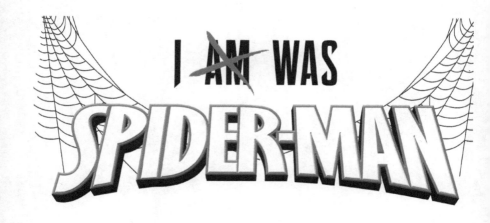

I ~~AM~~ WAS SPIDER-MAN

T0349372

BY: SCOTT LEVA

I AM/WAS SPIDER-MAN

Text Copyright © 2025 held by the author

Published in North America and Europe by Running Wild Press.
Visit Running Wild Publishing at www.runningwildpublishing.com

ISBN (ebook) 978-1-963869-12-5

ISBN (hardback) 978-1-963869-10-1

ISBN (paperback) 978-1-963869-11-8

"Scott Leva is by far the most creative Stunt Director in TROMA's 50 yrs of making money losing films... he we deserves his Stunt Oscar!! This book is entertaining and very informative for film fans and all of us."

— Lloyd Kaufman, President and Co-Founder of Troma Entertainment, American Film Director, Producer, Director, and Author including

"All I Need To Know About FILMMAKING I Learned From THE TOXIC AVENGER: The Shocking True Story of Troma Studios"

https://www.lloydkaufman.com/

"Scott Leva! This guy made me Wolverine!" - **Hugh Jackman**

"That was incredible. Leva? You must be Jewish." - **Mel Brooks**

"You look like Peter Parker. You are Spider-Man." - **Stan Lee**

"Do I know you?" - **Ray Liotta**

"You are exactly how I envisioned Spider-Man to be." - **Jack Kirby**

"Don't fuck up." - **Clint Eastwood**

A NOTE FROM THE AUTHOR

This book has been in the back of my mind for over 25 years. It started when I documented my push for the role of Spider-Man for The Cannon film that was never made. I am glad that I did not write that book as it has evolved into something so much more. I have had a personal relationship with Spider-Man / Peter Parker most of my life.

Out of everything I accomplished, and some would say it's a lot, even in some cases extraordinary, my connection with Spidey is to this day what I am best known for. I still get requests for autographs and even interviews.

Recently on social media platforms like Facebook and Instagram it has spread even wider. I have received messages from people I barely know that because of my work with Spider-Man it has left a positive imprint on their lives. Some have said that I influenced them to achieve goals in their work and personal life. This has been incredible for me. I am thrilled that my association and love for this iconic hero has made such a positive impact on so many people.

I am constantly hearing. "You should do a pod cast; you should do a You Tube channel; we would love to hear more stories from you. You should WRITE a book."

A book. A book?

Why not. So here we go. These are my stories. This is my relationship with Spider-Man, the people that created him, and help make me a part of who I am. Thanks to them, I Am, (Was) Spider-Man.

I hope you enjoy it and maybe get a little inspiration from it.

TABLE OF CONTENT

CHAPTER

One

BEGINNINGS

So, I assume the best place to start is the beginning. I was born in Frankfurt Germany. Military family. My father was in the Army, my mother was, well a mother during that time. I had two older siblings. We were all born a year apart. We lived there four years, then headed back to the USA. I saw an old 8mm film of us traveling back to the States on a ship. It looked cool.

We traveled a lot when I was growing up. AND when I say a lot, I mean a LOT. We moved every six months to a year. I was always "the new kid". In my lifetime I have traveled to 49 of the 50 states. Someday I need to go to Alaska, just to finish the set.

Years Go By, From Baby Through Toddler

Family Dinner

Going to Church (Yes, We Did That)

As much as we traveled, we would always stop in Texas and Louisiana. My grandparents, uncles and aunts were there. My parents instilled in me to cherish and value my grandparents. I have made sure to pass this on to my daughter as well.

Father's Mother Alice

Mother's Aunt Tots & Mother Audrey

Our Cousins & Us

Moving all over the United States may sound exciting, but far from it. Imagine always being the new kid and trying to make new friends. I was always going to a new school that was never where I last left off. Even with all my traveling, I am terrible with geography. More on this later.

Moving around so much made us (my brothers and me) more of a solitude trio. We all found our passions so to speak. Mine would come to me during a trip to the local drug store. The stores had a magazine/comic section. The comics were usually on a spinning rack.

I would turn the rack and see all sorts of colorful comic characters. The comic that stuck out to me almost immediately was (wait for it.)

The Amazing Spider-Man # 39 "How Green Was My Goblin!" written By Stan Lee and drawn by Johnny Romita.

Now. Some interesting trivia.

This was the first Spider-Man issue illustrated by John Romita. Stan Lee and Steve Ditko, the original artist and co-creator had a disagreement (or so the story goes) about the identity of the Goblin. For me, it was an exciting colorful comic. It was the first comic book I ever read. I was hooked. And, like so many other fans, I fully related to Peter Parker. It was a two-part story, and it would be a few years before I read the follow up. Mind you, I did not know these were monthly titles.
I read other issues. Issue 43 Rhino on The Rampage, 44, Where Crawls the Lizard, also a two parter. 46, The Shocker,47, Kraven, and so forth.

I also read other comics. But Marvel was my favorite. Stan Lee had his soapbox. A letters page, and even gave the crew cool nicknames. Jack (King Kirby). Jazzy Johnny Romita, and of course Smilin ' Stan Lee. I felt connected. I grew up during a time that Marvel comics became a pop icon. They had TV shows, toys, lunch boxes, and other cool fun things that are huge collector items worth a small fortune today. Who knew where it would be today, and what part I got to play in its history as well.

CHAPTER
Two

SCHOOLS PART 1

School was, and is, an important part of shaping who we can be, will be or ultimately are today. In my particular case, school or schools, I should say as I attended multiple schools most of my early years, not so much shaped me as strengthened me to become who I am today, in spite of some of the hurdles thrown at me during my formidable school years.

To quote Aristotle, "Those who Know, do. Those that understand, teach." Not to speak for ALL teachers, but a few I had neither knew much nor taught well.

Growing up and joining a new school on a consistent basis was probably the most difficult time of my life. My siblings as well. It was amazing we learned anything much less survived each school year.

I do not recall kindergarten. First grade was Mrs. Bell. She looked like the stereotypical Schoolmarm. First grade was relatively easy. My parents had this huge jar filled with pennies. They thought it would be a good incentive to award the jar to the child with the highest grade. Not a fair contest as I was in first grade, and my siblings were in second and third, as well as the fact it was a new school for them. I won the penny jar. My eldest sibling was very hurt. I still feel bad about this today.

I was given the penny wrappers to put the pennies in. They totaled fifty cents a roll. I mainly used them as blockades for my toy soldiers. And, in the end used my winnings to buy toys and candy. I wasn't really given much of an education on finances.

My 2nd grade teacher was Mrs. Finney (new school).

My siblings both wore glasses at the time and kept having me wear them as they thought I looked like one of their teachers Mr. Beard. It is my understanding that you should not wear prescription glasses if you do not need prescription glasses. It can mess up your sight.

Needless to say, I was starting to have vision issues. Mrs. Finney was very understanding and would have me move closer to the board. Shortly after she advised my parents of my eyesight issues.

So, I needed glasses. This was OK. Peter Parker originally wore glasses. And, there was of course Superman / Clark Kent. That was pretty cool. Plus, I looked smarter. However, nicknames like Four Eyes were not fun.

Before Glasses

After Glasses

Third grade was not too memorable. I forget the teacher's name. She was a bit short and angry with her comments at times. It too was new school. I had trouble keeping up. I remember not finishing my homework. Truthfully, I had too much stuff going on at home. However, when asked why, I thought I would be truthful. I said I did not feel like it. BIG mistake. All hell broke loose. Interesting enough, a few other students followed my lead and used the same excuse.

You would think they would have learned from my folly.
I had trouble academically in third grade. I almost did not advance to fourth grade. The teachers thought it would be in my best interest to be placed in fourth grade and see how that worked. What did it mean to be placed in the next grade? This occurs when a student is not doing the caliber of work that indicates the student should be promoted to the next grade. However, the Student Intervention Team recommended, and the building administrator concurred, that it was in my best interest to move to the next grade.

I may not have been as academically sharp as Peter Parker, but maybe I could make it up in physical abilities.

I do not fully recall most of my fourth-grade year, so I will move on.

Bowie Maryland.

My NEW nightmare began as I entered fifth grade. It was to be a whole new experience. One that I personally would never forget.

I remember walking into the classroom looking for an open seat. A few of the seats were open but the student sitting in front of or beside it would place their hand on the seat showing it as "OFF LIMITS".

After moving around a bit, the teacher, Mrs. Bloom, bellowed in, "Are you going to stand around all day like some fool, or are you going to sit already?"

There were snickers from the class. I found an empty seat near the back of the room. And so, we began...

The students were working on geography lessons. Now remember I mentioned earlier that geography was and still is my worst subject.

Mrs. Bloom asked students questions. Some could answer, some couldn't. She asked me a question. "What is the Capitol of Oklahoma?"

I was confused.

"Oklahoma? Hello. I thought you traveled a lot. Are you really that stupid, or did you just not pay attention when you lived all over the country?"

I was still confused. AND a bit embarrassed.

"Well?"

"I'm not sure."

"You're not SURE of what? If you're stupid or if you didn't pay attention?"

"I'm not sure what the Capitol of Oklahoma is."

"OK. We'll just say you didn't PAY attention. You better pay attention in my class. I will not put up with that in my class. Who in our classroom can tell him the answer?"

Hands went up as I stood very confused and slightly humiliated.

Various bits of cruelty happened. I was called names by the teacher. Yelled at. Just made miserable. I hated going to school.

One time, it was so bad I told my parents I was sick. I couldn't go to school that day. They did the parent thing, took my temperature, said I should go. I remembered crying so hard, that they finally said I could stay home. It was a fun day. Staying in bed. Reading my comics. It was a short reprieve.

I also remembered walking to and from school and seeing patrol boys with orange sashes and badges helping students at the crosswalk. I thought this was so cool. I became a patrol boy. I remembered proudly wearing my sash and badge to help students across the street. I was at my happiest then.

That was a short-lived time. In a few weeks, Mrs. Bloom would strike again. I do not remember what the question was, but I had difficulty with the answer. Mrs. Bloom made me turn in my Patrol Boy sash and badge, stating I was "too stupid to be a patrol boy."

I was humiliated again and again, both by the teacher and the students. I assumed the students would join in to avoid the wrath of Bloom (Rhymes with Doom.) At one point I remembered holding a painful smile on my face, while Mrs. Bloom berated me. She grabbed my face in her hands, shaking my head, and taunting me.

"What are you smiling about? You want to cry; you know you want to cry."

I finally broke down and cried. She told me to go clean up. I make her sick.

While I was in in the bathroom cleaning up an older boy asked me why I was crying. Too embarrassed to tell the truth I said I was beat up by a sixth grader.

When I got back to the classroom, Mrs. Bloom made fun of me for saying a sixth grader beat me up. The boy had obviously gone to my classroom to report the incident.

We had different classes we went to throughout the day. One had a teacher I really liked. He was attentive, and it was easy to feel safe in his class. At the end of the year I wrote him a letter expressing how much I enjoyed his class. I said I wish he were my regular teacher. I really liked him. I found out that he gave the letter to Mrs. Bloom. I no longer liked him after that.

I do not know why Mrs. Bloom had such an affinity towards me. It felt like outright hatred. I am sure throughout the years she treated other students this way.

Later on, when I was older, and I told my mother the story, she was horrified. Why did I not tell her then? As a child, we are taught to respect and listen to grown-ups in positions of authority. I thought I was doing something wrong. It is important that our children know to speak up. And it is important that the parents listen.

I have always wanted to make a short film about this time in my life. I have written some of the script. It is titled "Bloom in Spring". Hopefully someday soon, I will do this.

Again, sixth grade does not spark many memories. I recall being picked on a lot. I fought my way through most of that particular school year. Not sure what the issues were, but I don't remember a week going by that there wasn't some confrontation.

As I mentioned, we moved so much, that some of these times are a jumbled memory. There are times in my life that had a huge effect on me and are not easily forgotten.

CRESTVIEW ELEMENTARY SCHOOL
Mrs. Baker – Grade 6
1969   1970

CHAPTER
Three

TV SHOWS
THAT INFLUENCED ME

Like most families, we had television. I was always allowed after I got home from school to watch a few of my favorite shows, along with a snack before doing my homework.

Early on there was the Mickey Mouse Club. So much fun. The Adventures of Superman (George Reeves) before my time, but reruns. These were great moments of escape from the real world.

As time went by, my parents got us a color TV. This was awesome. The television world changed with color. So many shows would have that *In Color* before the show. The Wonderful World of Disney In LIVING color. Hosted by Walt Disney himself. I loved Disney.

And I loved Saturday morning cartoons. Top Cat, Huckleberry Hound. Hanna Barbara. So much to watch.

And, of course Marvel. The Marvel Superhero cartoon, that had moving pictures that looked like they were cut out of the comic book. It didn't matter. It was still cool.

But nothing compared to "The Amazing Spider-Man" TV Series. It was so exciting to see Spidey's comic book stories come to life. It didn't matter that his webbing was only on his mask, gloves and boots. It was great.

Those shows were fun, but the shows that had the most influence on me were "Batman", "Get Smart", "Mission Impossible". Don't get me wrong, I loved the fantasy, comedy shows. "I Dream of Jeannie", "Bewitched" and of course everyone loved "The Ed Sullivan Show".

But the other shows caught my interest. Especially, the main one, "The Wild, Wild West". My oldest sibling was a huge "Star Trek" fan. I was not. Interesting that that would become a big part of my future.

"The Wild, Wild West" was something else. It was James Bond in the West. James West and Artemus Gordon. Truthfully? The stunt team along with Robert Conrad could easily stand up to some Jackie Chan style action. Those guys took some major hits. Conrad was actually injured a few times. One stunt actually knocked him out.

I wanted to do that. There were many shows I would copy and play act. Thankfully I did not attempt to do big kick ass stunts at the time. (Don't try this at home.)

I recently started watching The Wild, Wild West again. It's funny how sexist, misogynistic, and sometimes racist the early shows were. They had quite a few paint downs with Indians and Asians. A "few" Black actors, Floyd Patterson, a famous boxer, and Gloria Calomee, to name a few, although this was later down the road. As well as a few Asian Americans. Mainly pretty women. This gave me whole new perspective. I still enjoyed the show. A book was published awhile back about the series. The Wild, Wild West the series by Susan Kesler. I went to a convention back in 2018 and the book had been reissued for its 30th anniversary. Quite a few of the original stunt crew were there. Whitey Hughs, Bob Herron, (Ross Martins' stunt double) Dick Cangey and Jim George (who doubled Robert Conrad). Also present was the producer Bruce Lansbury, Ross Martins' widow Olavee Martin and the author, Susan E. Kesler. Now, I was in the industry at the time, but became a bit of a fan boy and had all these people sign my copy.

THE
WILD
WILD
WEST
THE SERIES

BANK

By
Susan E. Kesler
Edited by Jude Bradley   Foreword by Bruce Lansbury

Now, these shows, as exciting as they were, did not instill in me the thought of being an actor. No. That would come later…

CHAPTER
Four

MOVIES
THAT INFLUENCED ME

The movies of my youth were pure classics. They stood the test of time. Movies like, The Godfather, Deliverance, Lawrence of Arabia. Incredible. Our big thing was Disney movies. "The Computer Wore Tennis Shoes", "The Absent-minded Professor". Fred MacMurray was a huge Disney star at the time, not to mention his hit TV series, "My Three Sons". One of his most endearing was "Follow Me Boys". Along with Kurt Russel, and Dean Jones, they were fun family entertainment.

But, not to digress. My favorite movies were and still are "Midnight Cowboy", "Taxi Driver", and "To Kill a Mockingbird". But the one that changed it all for me was "The Great Escape". Seeing Steve McQueen riding and jumping that motorcycle over the barbed wire fences was amazing. I did not know that such a profession as stuntmen existed then, nor that stunt legend Bud Ekins was his stunt double. I was hooked. THAT was what I wanted to do. Be an actor and do all that crazy fun action stuff.

In the previous chapter, I mentioned some of the stunt players that worked on "The Wild, Wild West". Quite a few were well known then and even today. Tommy Huff, Gene Lebell, And Terry Leornard to name a few. Victor Paul, a master swordsman was the stunt double for Burt Ward on "Batman". Buddy Van Horn doubled Guy Williams on "Zorro", and Jeannie Epper doubled Linda Carter on "Wonder Woman". Why am I mentioning these stuntmen and woman? Because in my career I have had the pleasure of meeting and working with many of these stunt legends. I would not be in business today if not for them.

The Boy Wonder: Victor Paul

Jeannie Epper

Buddy Van Horn

We will revisit this later.

After deciding that I wanted to be an actor, I started learning about the industry. Directors, actors, and writers. As time went on, I got into all types of movies. Movies directed by Steven Spielberg, Francis Ford Coppolla, John Huston and Martin Scorcesse. Stars like Robert Redford, Marlon Brando, Clint Eastwood, Robert De Niro, and Jack Nicholson.

Again, my career path made it possible to meet and even work with many of these screen icons.

All because of a little war movie called, "The Great Escape".

CHAPTER
Five

TOYS
THAT INFLUENCED ME

Toys were and are a wonderful escape into fantasy realms. They are fun, imaginative, and even educational. We give toys to new born babies, kittens and puppies, to name a few. For me, toys were a way to act out some of my favorite movies, TV shows, and comic books.

I had some cool toys. Some robots, a Godzilla type of plastic motorized toy that I shot rubber darts at. I had ventriloquist dummies. Jerry Mahoney, Charlie McCarthy, and few others I don't remember. I was very strong into Ventriloquism for a while. I took it very seriously. Read the books, listened to the records. Learned from the masters. Paul Winchell and Edgar Bergen. And of course, Shari Lewis with Lamb Chop.

Godzilla?

Expert Ventriloquist

Now, I played with other cool toys too but ventriloquism put me in the spotlight. I could actually improvise with my dummy pal. Many times, people watching would get into a conversation with the dummy. Actual arguments.

As I mentioned before, we moved a lot. Texas was our main hub. We seemed to go there the most, and my father's family was situated there.

So, during one time when we were in Texas, we were in an apartment complex. I had the Charlie McCarthy dummy sitting on the windowsill on a three-foot wall that easily hid me from view.

I could hear people walking by and I would shout out to them. One older boy, much bigger than me got into having a shouting match with my dummy. (Truthfully, who was the real dummy there?)

While threatening to beat my dummy up as I hurled very funny insults at him, my older brother walked in. As he neared the window, from the older boy's vantage point, it looked like he stood up behind the wall. As he came in the room and asked me what I was doing, I let the dummy fall against the window frame, and sit there. The boy below started threatening my brother. My brother was very defensive.

"It wasn't me, it was him!" as he pointed at me below the window sill. This looked like he was pointing at the now motionless dummy.

"I know it was you! Do you think I'm stupid? You were making him talk." (Referring to the dummy.)

My brother was adamant that it was not him, but the person he was pointing to. The older boy threatened him with a beating if he saw him outside of the apartment. I don't think my brother left the apartment for at least a week.

Outside of abusing my neighbors, I would do talent shows at school.

It was my first foray into entertainment.

Before, during, and after my ventriloquism time, I had other toys that I played with. "G.I. Joe, The Real American Hero". They had tons of accessories. Jeeps, space capsule, scuba gear and just about every military type imaginable.

HASBRO constantly updated the G.I. Joe line. New accessories. New figures.

Their line of foreign soldiers was the best. Australia, Britain, France, Japan, and of course Germany. I had to have the German soldier. I had no inkling of the war history at that time. Nazis, the holocaust, things like that. Today, these would most likely be considered politically incorrect. But I had to have a German soldier to fight my US soldier while he was on a motorcycle to reenact the great escape.

G.I. Joe

German G.I. Joe

So, HASBRO was the big toy company for young boys. They were top sellers. Ideal toys decided they wanted a piece of that market. They came up with their own 12-inch action figure. Captain Action. Captain Action would change into my favorite comic hero. Superman, Batman Aquaman, Captain America, Sgt Fury, Steve Canyon, Flash Gordon, The Lone Ranger and the Phantom. They were a hit. Like G.I. Joe, they started to get add ons. A sanctuary, that I believe was a Sears exclusive. The Silver Streak car. So cool. Then the new costumes came out. Tonto, Buck Rogers, The Green Hornet, and of course my favorite, Spider-Man. It was a Steve Ditko version of the suit. Not to leave the girls out, Ideal also came out with a line of super heroine dolls. Super Queens. Wonder Woman, Bat Girl, and Mera. Captain Action got a side kick Action Boy who would change into Robin, Superboy and Aqua Lad. And of course, no hero was complete without a villain. Introducing Dr. Evil. A blue alien type of character that wore the disguise of a scientist. All the rerelease costumes came with a flicker ring.

Captain Action

Action Boy

DC Comics did a comic book illustrated by Gil Kane. Aurora Models that also did Spider-Man, Hulk, Captain America, Batman, Superman, Wonder Woman, as well as a slew of TV and movie figures did Captain Action. The big seller was if you wanted all your heroes together you would have to get another Captain Action figure to be that hero.

I was in comic heaven. These toys were worth a small fortune a few years back. A new company, Playing Mantis came out with an updated release. Added a few extra costumes. Kato, Romita style Spidey. Dr. Evil got some cool villains as well. Something we always wanted.
I think after the new release the prices dropped on the vintage ones. Out of nostalgia, I bought some of the new releases.

Endless hours I played superhero adventures. Spider-Man was always the main hero.

Vintage Ditko Style

New Romita Style

Tons of toys that catered to young boys at the time. Major Mat Mason, Johnny West, Hot Wheels. Just about anything that would cater to the male adrenaline rush.

Johnny West

I still have fond memories of these toys. A long time ago during my time working for Marvel doing Spider-Man appearances, I was reintroduced to vintage Captain Action figures at comic and toy conventions. I got into collecting Captain Action toys and accessories. About three years and $11,000.00 dollars, I had a full boxed and unboxed collection of everything. It was exciting.

I would get people in touch with me that wanted to trade or sell. At one point, this person in San Diego California got in touch with me. He had some boxed and unboxed Captain Action figures and costumes. He wanted $500.00 for the whole lot. No haggling. I asked what he had. He mentioned Captain America, boxed with Ring. Captain Action with Parachute, Flash Gordon with Ring, all of which I had. Loose figures, costumes, oh. And Dick Tracy. "what"? Dick Tracy. There was no Dick Tracy. I was pretty sure he was talking about one of the rarest boxed costumes at that time. One that sold for $2,000.00. I said I would be there the next day. When I arrived. He had all the items. And, oh. Not Dick Tracy. The Green Hornet. I had found the Holy Grail that completed my collection.

It was a small collectors' group at that time. I let all my collector friends know what I had. It was rare.

One day, I got a call from a collector that had received my information from another collector friend of mine.

"I hear you have the Green Hornet in the box."

"Yes."

"How much do you want for it?"

"It's not for sale."

He would check in on a weekly basis. Same conversation.

One day he called again. "What would it take for you to part with it?"

I said $5,000.00 expecting that would end the back and forth.

There was a pause.

Would you take a cashier's check?

I was stunned. What the heck, we made a deal.

After that transaction, it officially became the end of my collecting Captain Action. Over the next few months, I sold everything.

My initial three and half years of investment that cost me about $11,000.00 made me a whopping $35,000.00. Quite a turn around on my investment.

A side story that I will get more into later, I got into collecting 1/6 scale figures later on. I still have most of them.

Not Dick Tracy

CHAPTER
Six

SCHOOLS PART 2

Junior high school through high school was like with most people, a true learning and living experience. I started to form friendships and started to become VERY interested in girls.

"Seventh grade we moved again..."

Distinguished Flying Cross

AWARDED FOR ACTIONS
DURING Vietnam War

Service: Army
Rank: Major

GENERAL ORDERS:

Headquarters, 1st Aviation Brigade, General Orders No. 2260 (April 17, 1968)

CITATION:

The President of the United States of America, authorized by Act of Congress, July 2, 1926, takes pleasure in presenting the Distinguished Flying Cross to Major (Field Artillery) Neil I. Leva (ASN: 0-81479), United States Army, for heroism while participating in aerial flight, evidenced by voluntary actions above and beyond the call of duty while serving with the 189th Assault Helicopter Company, 1st Aviation Brigade, in the Republic of Vietnam, on 6 February 1968. Major Leva distinguished himself by exceptionally valorous actions while serving as Aircraft Commander of an unarmed helicopter on a recovery mission to evacuate a helicopter shot down by enemy fire. The downed helicopter was located outside the perimeter of a firebase and was under fire by the enemy. He unhesitatingly landed in close proximity to the downed aircraft and went to it in order to determine whether it was capable of flying out. Immediately, he and his crew were fired upon by enemy mortars. He continued to check the aircraft and determined it to be capable of flying. He returned to his helicopter and took off. After directing armed helicopters onto the enemy mortar positions, he landed again by the downed aircraft. After completing the necessary preparations for the aircraft's flight under enemy mortar fire, he waved the pilot off and returned to his ship. Despite damage by enemy fire, the downed aircraft was saved as he also flew out of the area under fire after accomplishing his mission successfully. His heroic actions were in keeping with the highest traditions of the military service and reflect great credit upon himself, his unit, and the United States Army.

Back to Texas. Killeen Texas to be exact. Fort Hood where my father was battalion commander. A brief synopsis about my father. As far back as I can remember he was a Military Man. Army. He was a pilot, both small engine planes and helicopters. He did two tours of Duty in Vietnam. One of which he was injured under fire and received the Purple Heart. He also received the Distinguished Flying Cross for an incredible act of bravery.

My Father with His Adopted Pet Mongoose

He would be gone for what seems like forever. As with most parents, children can have issues with their father or mother. I had issues. But I can say he tried. He taught and supported me as well as he could. So, he was the best father he could be. That is saying a lot.

Now Killeen Texas was mainly a military city, as a lot of the students lived on the base with their military family. It was pretty much the same ole same ole for me. Trying to acclimate. Trying to fit in.

I made friends. Todd was a decent kid, but to show his superiority, there was a time (out of the blue) he wanted to fight me. I refused. So, for almost a month, I avoided him. I rode my bike to school instead of taking the bus.

One day crossing the field to my home, Todd and his "entourage" met me head on. I refused to engage. Todd grabbed my handlebars and refused to let go. I dropped the bike and walked away. The next day, I decided to deal with my "bully" friend head on. I took the bus.

As we were going home, I heard the other boys whispering to Todd. As we got off the bus, Todd called my name. I stopped, clenched my fists, and turned to face him. To my surprise, he apologized. And in the end, we became friends again. Good thing too. We were on the same football team. This was reminiscent of Peter Parker being bullied during his school day. Todd would have been my Flash Thompson.

Todd Is Number 72, I Am Sitting Directly to the Left of Him

There was a girl I liked as well. Our families were friends. Later when we moved, I met her again. We both realized we had unspoken crushes on each other. But, that was then. We never became more than friends.

However. My best friend was a boy named Ross Hudson. We became close. We did everything together. G.I. Joe was still big then and we used to play with those as well. We rode bikes, and pretty much did what best buddies would do.

Ross had Leukemia. His mother spoke to me about it. He would need to have treatments. I did not fully understand the severity of this. Ross was just like everyone else. He told me one day on the bus, that he would most likely die from this. I did not take him too seriously.

The biggest bond that Ross and I had were our love of comics. Ross was a huge Captain America Fan. Me? Well Spider-Man of course. I actually received the coveted No Prize for answering some obscure question. I was a true Marvelite.

The Coveted No Prize

We would seek hard to find issues of our heroes trying to complete our collection. A special issue came out at the time. All the Marvel comic books had this king-sized book. Spider-Man was #102. Captain America was #143. I was lucky to get my Spider-Man issue. Ross, not so much. During that time, pre-internet and comic stores on every corner, when you missed an issue it was not so easy to find it.

I used to go to the movies every weekend. I would bring some comics to read. There was an older boy who sat a few rows back. He would ask to borrow a comic to read as well. At the end of the movie, I would go out front and he would be there and return my comic.

One day I found a copy of the elusive Captain America #143 that Ross wanted so much. I was on my way to the movies. I figured I would read it and see what all the excitement Ross had about Cap was. And, at the theatre, the older boy asked to borrow it. I told him that it was a very important comic, so be careful.
At the end of the movie, I went out front as usual. No sign of the boy. I went back inside. Nothing. For the first time the boy kept the comic. A special book that Ross wanted so bad.

Ross was very upset to say the least. Ross never got that comic. It really bothered me a lot, as we moved again. I never saw Ross again, and shortly after we moved, I was told Ross passed away. This still hurts a bit today.

I do not remember much of 8th grade. But 9th?

Nineth was the turning point of my life.

We moved to California.

Huntington Beach. I went to Marina High School. I enrolled in Drama class with Bob Myers as my teacher. I was in all the plays. I liked the school. I liked the teachers, and I got my first serious girlfriend, Karen.

The summer of '73 was exciting and fun. My world revolved around Karen. Having a girlfriend gave me confidence and feelings of strength and maturity. I rode my bike everywhere. Especially to her house. I was probably in the best shape of my life at the time.

I had biker's legs.

My dream was still wanting to be an actor. As I said earlier, I was in all the school plays. "Teahouse of the August Moon", "Dames at Sea", a few I forget.

I enrolled in a summer theatre program. Karen was a part of it as well. We were going to perform the play, "The Secret Life of Walter Mitty". We rehearsed a bit, but not as much as we should have. I was playing Walter Mitty. We spent a lot of our time building sets and dealing with wardrobe.

As the opening night grew closer, I realized that I was not fully prepared. I was not 100% sure of my dialogue. Thankfully, the school had a blackout and the play was cancelled. The real fun was working as crew. I admit, being the lead did give me a bit of an attitude, that thankfully I outgrew pretty quickly. I learned the value of working as a team.

At the end of the school year Mr. Myers held a small party and rewards ceremony. Rewards were given out for various accomplishments. I was told by a few classmates that I was going to receive one as well.

As the rewards were given out, names called, I sat there seeing what looked like every certificate and plaque given out. I was disappointed. Then, the final reward. Don't remember the exact category, but I heard my name. It was a beautiful theatre trophy similar to the Tony. It was an incredible moment that I will always cherish. He was a kind and generous teacher. I had the pleasure of seeing him again many years later after I was successful in the entertainment industry. It was a kind of reunion. He was happy to see me, and I was surprised he remembered me. Good memories.

With Bob Myers at Our School Reunion

My romance with Karen was pretty short lived. We did not break up. I moved again.

This time to Maryland. I was hurt and I was angry. It was an anger that lasted quite a while.

I stayed in touch with Karen, but we slowly moved apart. She visited for a week, but things changed. She had a new boyfriend. I heard her say I love you when she was talking with him on the phone. I was devastated.

This only fueled my anger.

I started at a new high school, Wootton High. I met new friends, had new girlfriends, and sort of muddled my way through high school.

Again, I was in all the plays. Two seniors were getting all the roles. I do not remember the boy's name, but the girl was Jackie. She was an amazing talent. She played Annie in Annie Get Your Gun. She belted the songs like a young Ethel Merman. We did the Music Man. I was one of the traveling salesmen along with chorus. The term, "there are no small parts, only small actors" rings true. I was thrilled to be in the plays. It was my first real theatre experience, and I loved just being a part of any production.

When my junior year came along and the previous senior class had graduated, I started getting the leading roles. Plays like, "Rally Round the Flag Boys", "George Washington Slept Here" and "The Odd Couple".

We had a media room as well. We could check out the equipment. Use the camera, and even edit. It was a learning experience. It made me have a positive interest in film making and was instrumental in my wanting to learn more about every aspect of production. When I was a professional working sets I would ask a ton of questions about camera set ups, lens, effects, you name it.

I decided to do my take on the Old George Reeves "The Adventures Of Superman" TV series for class. It was a lot of fun, my dad helped with the costume. We even used flying clips from the actual show. I remember that the class really liked it.

I wanted to do a Spider-Man, but by the time the costume was finished, that class was over, so I wore the Spidey suit for Halloween and Gordon wore the Superman.

We had a blast driving around town and doing fun heroic things for people. At one point a person's car was stalled, so the other person in our car offered to help, and said, no this is a job for superheroes. At first, he thought our friend was crazy until he saw us come out and help him push his car to the side of the road. The car owner had a great laugh. This was incredible, he laughed, "This is so great!" High school antics.

Gordon was a good friend. We liked a lot of the same things. He and I would hang out together a lot. Moving around as much as I did, I did not have any real relationships, much less close friends, so this was a new experience for me. His father had committed suicide and Gordon became distant. I understood this as it was a shock. I did not really know his family that well. So I don't know the exact details to what might have led up to this. I recently learned from a Facebook post that Gordon had passed away. I am sorry we lost touch.

Mrs. Janet Schwinger was both our English teacher and our Drama teacher. I liked her. She had a huge enthusiasm for theatre. It was contagious. She talked about theatre and drama like it was magical, so it became magical to me as well.

For some reason or other, I do not recall, she was replaced by Mr. Brodsky during my senior year. Mr. Brodsky did not particularly care for me. I don't know why. I did not perform in any of the plays after he took over.

I was still strong on movies then. Action movies in particular. I was part of the gymnastics team led by Coach Marion Griffin. She was also the dance choreographer for all the school musicals.

I learned a lot. I think all the boys that were in her class had some sort of crush on her.

My big turnaround was getting into Kung Fu. There was of course the TV series with David Carradine. But the big thing was, and to a point still is, Bruce Lee. He changed the way we looked at Kung Fu action. By the time I became really familiar with him and his work, he died. This only made him greater.

I worked hard at Kung Fu, and with the help of gymnastics really became a force to be reckoned with. Since I was the new kid a lot of the time, it made me a target. Kung Fu gave me an awareness and confidence that I still carry with me to this day. My Kung Fu school was Lin's Kung Fu. I even competed. It was thrilling to go to martial arts competitions. Won a few of the "Forms" events. This is like Katas in Karate. Doing certain movements that showed your skills. Excelling in Martial Arts gives you confidence. I also mastered the spin kick that Bruce Lee made famous. Pretty decent with weapons as well. It definitely helped me get more secure and stronger. Not Spider-Man stronger, but kind of the same feeling he might have had when he realized his powers.

GYMNASTICS

GYMKHANA: FIRST ROW: D. Rahn; Ms. Griffin, sponsor; L. Mason; J. Bray; S. Swaney; D. Cantor; J. Prescott; J. Kalimon; P. Putnam; A. Gardner; SECOND ROW: C. Theodore, C. Nelson, D. Danaceau, J. Edwards, K. Subotnik; THIRD ROW: G. Graham, K. Mackie, R. White, J. Dickson, J. Nangle, J. Jordy, T. Menke, T. Steiner, J. Prescott, A. Mackay, S. Leva, C. Celano, M. Pliska; FOURTH ROW: M. Alexander, A. Marvin, S. Vogan; not pictured: M. McCormick.

It was incredible.

I also started getting a reputation in school. "Mr. Kung FU". I was no longer bullied but feared.

I realized the change in how I was perceived when my middle brother came home from going to college in Texas. He took me aside and said he heard references to me as "Mr. Kung Fu". He told me that I might want to tone it down.
He was concerned that someday a kid might come to school with a gun to take me out. Now, we did not have major school shootings then like we do now, but we did have a few incidents, including one where a popular student had been killed.

I took his advice to heart and backed off. I made sure to only do my Kung Fu at the Kung Fu school.

After graduating high school, I was looking into college and some of the colleges I wanted to go to were not affordable. My parents had decided to no longer pay for college as my brothers were not doing well, and they no longer wanted to invest in our further education.

WOOTTON HIGH SCHOOL
Graduation
June 11, 1976

Being the youngest and last to go to college with a small budget
made my choices limited. I ended up going to Montgomery College
which was a community college that was well within my budget.
I paid for my own college. Had side jobs to make money, and still
living at home took away needing to pay for food and lodging. I had
a little resentment that when it came my time to go to college, my
parents changed the "paying for education rules". In their defense,
they were not extremely wealthy and school for three children can
be expensive.

CHAPTER
Seven

COLLEGE & DREAMING

I enjoyed my college years. School plays again. Some of which I played the lead. I was part of the gymnastics team, including competitions. I enjoyed the gymnastics competitions. I mainly did the floorwork like backhand springs, flips, and all around tumbling. I won a few. Most of our wins were for team points.

Gymnastics is probably one of the best skills you can have for stunt work. Your overall air sense, and coordination skill is perfect for doing falls and jumps for movies. This was definitely an asset for me, as well as for my future work as Spider-Man.

Some of which I added to my theatre roles. One of the first plays I auditioned for was "The Importance of Being Ernest" by Oscar Wilde. I was the new student, and there was already an established group of student actors from the previous year.

At the time I was going through my Robert Redford phase. Also, because my serious girlfriend in high school liked me this way, I dyed my hair blonde. Along with a flawless English accent, and a stand out audition, I was cast as Algernon Moncrief. Supposedly this was unheard of for a newbie to land a lead role. However, the entire cast and crew was very welcoming, and I was inducted into the Montgomery College Theatre group.

I do not fully remember the audition. I had to sign up for it. I read the play, and on the day, I recall auditioning with some of the older students who had been there a year or two before me. They were all impressed. I did not expect a large role, I assumed I would get a smaller part being the "new kid". When I got the role, I remember they welcomed me aboard with open arms. It was exciting. Usually being "the new kid" was a disaster. This was a nice change.

'Ernest' looking great at Montgomery College

By Jean Alexander
Sentinel Staff Writer

Montgomery College Drama Workshop has modernized "The Importance of Being Ernest" somewhat, bringing it from 1895 up to 1930, with period costumes and silver and white settings for Algernon's townhouse morning room and Jack's country house garden. Director Ed Sandler and his cast provide style and manners to match Oscar Wilde's witty lines, and "Ernest" has never looked better.

Jack and Algy are still the indolent, beautifully turned out young men about town enamored of two charming, completely vacuous young ladies. They are loved in return only because each girl believes her darling is called Ernest, a name that inspires the perfect trust and confidence that any well-bred girl insists on when considering candidates for matrimony.

Scott Leva and Michael Siegel play Algy and Jack, and Ellen Stokes and Dale Weisenfeld Gwendolyn and Cecily. Joan Puglisi's Lady Bracknell is the quintessence of social snobbery. Joseph Normile's Dr. Chasuble is a devastating caricature of a country rector. Gayle Abramowitz plays Miss Prism and Tony Souza and David Rothman butle away like crazy as Lane and Merriman.

Credit for sets and carefully researched costumes for "Ernest" goes to Donato Moreno, for lights to Emmitt Woodey, and for sound to Jim Adams.

"The Importance of Being Ernest" is a very special comedy that one always looks forward to seeing again. When it is as well done as it is here, it is a real treat. Don't miss it. Performances will be given by the Drama Workshop in the Fine Arts Theatre on the Montgomery College Rockville Campus at 8 p.m. Oct. 13 through 15 and at 7 p.m. Oct. 16. Tickets are $3.50 at the door or call 424-4416 for reservations.

Timely budget

The State of Maryland operates on $324,083,068 a month — $74,788,400 a week — $10,654,786 a day — $443,952 an hour — $7,399 a minute — $123 a second.

The classes were fun. The plays were well done. Almost professionally. I saw quite a few newspaper reviews that would praise Montgomery College's Theatre Program. Even saying it was better than some of the bigger universities. That was neat.

It was an exciting time of my life.

My gymnastics coach, Jon Jarboe, who I had a lot of respect for told me I needed to make a commitment. Gymnastics or theatre. It was difficult to balance practice and rehearsal.

So, I chose gymnastics. The next play was "The King and I". The lead was Michael Siegel, who played Jack Worthington in "The Importance of Being Ernest". A very talented man. He currently resides in the U.K. and is an acting teacher along with being in some plays, TV shows, and movies there. One of his cult classics was a part in "Killer Klowns from Space".

But, even with gymnastics I was still drawn to the theatre. I was asked to train one of the lead dancers on how to jump onto the stage off of a mini trampoline. So, in between gymnastics practice, I worked with him. He wanted to do a front flip onto the stage. I explained the danger as a cumbersome large mask would be too heavy and even somewhat difficult to see through.

Yet, the dancer after a lot of practice, decided to attempt it. I was not there at the time but was called in later as he had broken his ankle on the landing.

I was asked to fill in for him, and so I learned the dance, and easily performed the high-flying entrance.

With that the theatre beckoned.

The next play was Shakespeare's "A Midsummer Night's Dream". I was cast in dual roles. As Oberon, King of the Fairies (don't laugh) and Theseus the King of the Realm. The idea was that the characters were IDs of each other. The woman playing my wife was a teacher and even though considerably older than me, she was spot on.

It was a major turning point in my theatrical dreams. The director had brought in a friend that was a "professional" stuntman. Eric Pederson was there to help us with certain action scenes. This was exciting for me.

———————— March 1, 1978   The MC-Rockville Sour   Page 5

Leva Protrays Dual
Roles in 'Midsummer'

by Amy Nemitz

Scott Leva, a fourth semester student at Montgomery College, is starring in the play "A Midsummer Night's Dream," directed by Will Bellias.

Scott portrays a dual role: Duke Thesus (Lord of Athens) and Oberon (King of the Fairies). "The part itself is sensational," commented Leva. "At first the characters were very hard to portray, but now they're beginning to fall into place."

Scott adds, "Oberon is a character that a lot of people want to relate to. He's a neat character, who could be classified as a super being. Will Bellias gave the whole play a 'Frank Frazetta' style, which in itself is beautiful to behold."

Leva feels very positive about the play. "The play is very athletic. It's 'the most' exciting play I've ever been in," says Scott.

Besides acting, Leva enjoys tumbling and drawing, and is Spiderman for public appearances. He is very active with the gymnastics team. Leva is a very athletic person and is glad he can perform some of his skills in the play.

They have employed a professional stunt man, 'Eric Pederson', who will choreograph the aerobatics which in themselves are worth the admission. They have also employed 'Dianto Moreino', who is designing the set and costumes for the play.

Before a performance, Leva is very calm. It's when the curtain is raised the nerves begin to flair. After the first pangs of nervousness subside, he enjoys the character, the audience and the play.

A Midsummer Night's Dream begins on March 2nd and will close on March 5th.

"I'd like to go to Hollywood and act in movies and television, preferably movies," he says concerning his future plans.

"A Midsummer Night's Dream is an experience that can help me in the future and I wouldn't trade it for anything," concluded Leva.

Photo by Greg Collins

Scott Leva, one of the stars in "A Midsummer Nights' Dream."

Now my plan was always to go to New York. I traveled there from time to time. I wanted to be on Broadway. What aspiring actor didn't?

I had girlfriends through most of high school and college. A few made a lasting impact on my life. Looking back, I wish I had treated them better. My career and dreams had always taken precedence over everything else. I was not always there for them, nor was I always faithful.

I feel bad for many of the stupid things I did, and that my actions hurt someone. It was so uncalled for.

I am truly sorry for my inconsiderate and selfish actions.

As I said, I had a lot of anger during most of my time in Maryland. Most of it had been directed at my parents. We lived in a cookie cutter style home in Rockville, Maryland. All the houses looked identical. When we moved there, I remember driving down Dundee Road and my father proudly exclaiming, "Guess which house is the Leva's?" You could not tell them apart, and truthfully at that point I could care less. The houses were barely finished. It was a nightmare. It did not help with my anger issues.

In her defense, my mother was trying to make a stable home for us. (I did not know this at the time). My father was stationed at the pentagon. He was given an opportunity to transfer to Korea. I remember my mother saying that he was welcome to, but that we would not be going with him. It was basically an ultimatum. You choose. The Army or us. My mother had gone back to college. She received her degree in psychiatric social work and was quite a successful therapist.

My father decided to retire from the Army. Sadly, I was the only family member that attended his retirement.

With the family's support, he went back to school and also became a therapist.

That was the beginning of the end for them.

Now, my mother had found a great deal on this spectacular home in the Potomac. She bought it and decided that we were going to move.

I was livid. I was not going to move anymore. This was one of the final proverbial straws that set-in motion for me to move to New York.

At this point, with college, Kung Fu, and gymnastics, I was also an avid comics fan. Especially with Spider-Man. It was a sore point in most of my relationships. Some of my girlfriends did not like my love of comic books. Spider-Man in particular. Not sure why. Maybe they thought it was "nerdy". Or maybe they felt that all my attention should be focused on them.

I had a comic store that I frequented in Gaithersburg Maryland. The store was not doing well.

I suggested the owner have a promotion and have a Marvel character make an appearance. He thought it would be a great idea but wasn't sure of the cost.

So, I did some research. I was able to get information about Marvel Promotions. I called the head of Marvel Promotions, Nancy Allen. She informed me of the cost. $1,000.00 per day, plus transportation and hotel.

What if you had a local Spider-Man to make the appearance? I dunno, like me?

Well. I would have to go to New York and interview. It so happened they were having an actor/ character orientation the following week. I decided to fly in for the day.

I flew to LaGuardia. Took a cab and went to 575 Madison Avenue. MARVEL COMICS. I met Nancy and the other ladies working on promotions. I was told I was a bit short to play Spider-Man. I was 5'10" 165 pounds of gymnastics muscular frame.

I was told that, "Spider-Man is a fictional comic book superhero characterized by his iconic red-and-blue webbed body suit. Spider-Man is 5 feet 10 inches tall, weighs 167 pounds and has brown hair."

So, I put on the spandex Spidey suit which had been made by Eaves Brookes. One piece, zipper in the back along the place where the red meets the blue. White mesh eyes that made it very difficult to see, especially in a well-lit room.

I walked in.

Very Steve Dikto-ish in Spider-stature.

I leapt up onto the desk, back flipped off, and landed in a Ditko style Spidey pose.

The suit gave me confidence.

I was told to sit in the orientation. It dealt with proper ways to play the characters and how to handle difficult questions.

"Can you throw your Shield (Captain America). Shoot a web. How do you go to the bathroom?"

At the end we were told to introduce ourselves and say what character we played. Most were Spider-Man, a few Captain Americas. Hulk with a balloon style suit. Maybe a few others. It was still relatively new, and Spidey was the main sell. When it came to my turn, I said my name, but looked confused.

Nancy said "Spider-Man", so I guess I was officially hired.

Then I caught a flight back to Maryland and waited a long time before my first appearance.

I was still living in Maryland when I got the call from Barbara Maier. I was booked to play Spidey at a mall in Wilmington Delaware. I had to drive myself there, would be reimbursed for gas and travel. Food as well. Hotel. A WHOPPING $50.00 for the performance day. I was in heaven.

The appearance was a hit. I was very popular. And was on *Marvel's List*.

Now back to home life and anger. My mother set up for us to move to this incredible house with a ton of land, a barn on the property filled with old tires, and room to spare. I was not happy.

I was dating a nice Jewish girl at the time. Wendy. Very demanding. Had our whole future planned out for us. My family was not fond of her.
Our family always had pets. Pets were a big influence on my life as well. More about that later. We used to have a Siamese cat. Lynx. Lynx was beautiful. Did not like me too much as I was a bit too rough with her. We lost Lynx early on when we moved to Maryland. I was in the room when she was put down. I felt that no matter what our history, someone should be with her in the end. I'm glad I did.

My mother, my siblings and our pets, Cindy, Henry and Lynx

CHAPTER
Eight

NY, NY IT'S A WONDERFUL TOWN...

Before moving to New York City, I called Marvel Promotions. Barbara told me there would be more available work once I was local. I did not fully prepare. I thought I had a steady job, Fifty dollars did not go far in New York. I had a hotel apartment that rented by the month on West 45th street. Easy. Convenient. $250.00 a month. I was going to use my savings.

Once I set in my mind that I was going to move to New York, I got a full time job. I worked for Pinkerton Security in the Washington DC area. Yes. That Pinkertons. From the Wild West. As I understand it, they were founded around the mid 1880s to handle the more difficult outlaws. They were portrayed in various Western movies and TV shows including "Butch Cassidy and the Sundance Kid". So, I guess you can say I was a part of history. We wore security uniforms similar to police uniforms. I would bring my kitten with me and he would stay in my large desk drawer. During rounds where I would have to clock in at each location he would go with me. Running around, hiding behind parking lot pillars. He was so cool. More like a dog than a cat. It was an easy job. Nothing out of the ordinary ever happened. I took on extra shifts. Big overtime. Saved all my money.

Now, obviously this was not my first job. I worked at Toys "R" Us for a while. Shipping and receiving. It was cool, because they were stocking the eight-inch Mego toys. I got them all. Marvel, DC, Star Trek, and even Planet of the Apes. So working in a toy store would fuel my comic hero appreciation. My best friend, Gordon Lynn, worked there as well. We would play around too much. There was a loud speaker unit we used to call for in store help with employees. If I did not release the button, I would hear the other employee over the loud speaker. Once, I was playing around, and Gordon cussed. A few choice words not suitable for a family toy store. We were fired.

I also worked at a snack stand by the pool at Lakewood Country Club. This was a summer job. The next year I convinced the head boss to let me be the manager. He agreed. Big mistake. It was a full-time job. 24 / 7. One day I had everything set up with sandwiches ready for pick up in the main dining room for an event. Everything was plug and play. So, I took my first day off in weeks.

Later that day I got a call from head management. The sandwiches were not picked up. My employees were having a food fight at the snack bar. I hurried over, took care of everything, and stayed the rest of the day.

I was fired. The person I left in charge who was the main culprit, was made manager. She apologized, but what was done was done.

I did learn more about being professional when doing these jobs. So that was something. Definitely had a fun professional outlook when doing Marvel Spider-Man promotions, so I guess, "A lesson well learned."

And finally, before I took the job with Pinkerton, I worked construction. I learned a lot. It was actually kind of fun. This came in handy later in New York as well.

Now, back to New York. My first night there I walked down

Broadway. Looked at all the theatres. The stores. Times Square. Times Square was very seedy at the time, but I did not care.

Broadway lights.

The hotel apartments were similar to the one Jon Voight's' character Joe Buck lived in the movie, "Midnight Cowboy". That was cool as it was one of my favorite movies. Still is.

I started doing the rounds. I got good response to my auditions. I needed better head shots. I went to a photography studio. I was a bit strapped for cash, but, as luck would have it, they needed a small changing room. I offered to build the room in exchange for photos. My construction work came in handy. The new photos helped as they were more professional and looked more like my current me.

Got my pictures. Started getting weekly editions of "Backstage", an industry trade publication. It covered the film and performing arts industry from the perspective of performers, unions, and casting. And the Ross Reports—a bi-monthly directory of talent agents, casting directors, and casting calls, and other casting resources.

I immediately started submitting to casting agents. And, lo and behold, I actually started getting calls. Feuer & Ritzer were the premier casting agents in New York. They called me in for an audition for a well know film called The Warriors. I was supposed to meet with the producers. As I sat patiently at Paramount Plaza, Howard Feuer came out and told us the role had been cancelled. He thanked us and promised he would keep us in mind for future castings.

I was disappointed, but figured, what the heck. Next time.

I got calls from various soap operas. I did extra work at first. One time, there was a group of us background extras working out in a gym scene. They were adamant about being on camera. I could care less. Whenever the camera was being set up they would move to a spot that assured them they would be on camera. I would stay on my own, just doing background workout. But the director liked what I was doing and decided to open the shot on me, the other background actors started to move towards me to get in the shot. I remember getting ready to tell them to back off, but the director beat me to it. I knew casting pretty well. They liked me, and I think my "close up may have led to Under 5 work," which is a role with five lines or less.

I got involved in the theatre community. I would read the local trade papers and audition for just about any and all productions. I started to get to know most of the theatre owners and was becoming a part of that community. Off, off Broadway. And I would check in with Marvel. Luckily my weekends were full doing Marvel Promotions.

Now the truth is, I was very naïve. I did not know the business well, and many of the things I got were through dumb luck. I also made my fair share of mistakes. More about that as well.

I was fortunate to work on the "Superman" movie as background. There I met the main stunt coordinator in New York, Alex Stevens. He took a liking to me and made me his protégé. I got to work on some of the New York action scenes because of him. I'm in the scene where Lois jumps out of the Daily Planet window to prove Clark is Superman. He uses his heat vision and gets a fruit stand canopy to act like a net. I was on set during some of the flying sequences. There was a black out in New York but by using movie lights the show went on.

The first day I saw Chris Reeve as Superman was monumental. He came out of his trailer, wardrobe, placed his cape on by tying it under his arms under his suit. Seeing him walk onto the set-in full Superman regalia was a comic fans dream come true. He WAS Superman.

In the final movie cut, when Clark first came to the Planet in a taxi, you can see me in the crowd scene walking by the Daily Planet building. Don't blink.

Now, as much as I liked Alex, my goal was to be an actor, so I basically moved on and pursued that. However, my initial dumb luck was drying up, and I was running out of money.

Through *Backstage* I was finding auditions for low budget movies. One I auditioned for was a cult classic called, "Mother's Day". I did not get the part, but I was able to finagle stunt work.

The director was Charles Kaufman. His brother was Lloyd Kaufman one of the heads of TROMA films. They would become a large part of my future.

Now this was 1979. I was taking a stage fight class headed by Allen Suddeth. Good guy. Very knowledgeable. I learned how to throw a stage punch, make a hitting sound called a knap.
He also taught weapon work.

This was helpful to me in working out the action on a film that I had no qualifications or business to be a stunt coordinator on. It made it easier to choreograph action with a stage fight and gymnastics background. So, because of this training, I did not go in completely unprepared.

We worked in a wooded area that looked like a campground with bungalows for *Mother's Day*. They had separate accommodations for the crew and actors. Just across the lake they were filming another horror film, *Friday the 13th*. One of the actresses on our film, Debra, also worked for Marvel Promotions. She played Spider-Woman.

It was a fun movie. I was able to put together some cool action sequences that actually worked. My gymnastics background was extremely useful in falling down hills and jumping out of a second story window onto mattresses. I even set up a stunt that made it look like the actor was smacked hard in the face with a tree branch.

I did have an inherent self-preservation about safety. That was part of the need to plan things out. One of the actors was being too rough and Debra would complain about it. The actor did not fully grasp the concept. There was a vicious rape sequence that in the end I doubled for the actor at Debra's request. It was difficult, but that's show biz.

The director was looking at the possibility of a more dramatic death for one of the villains. I looked into a fire stunt. I knew that I needed cotton clothing, and actually got in touch with Marvel to get one of their older Spider-Man costumes that was all cotton, and not spandex, to test out the fire. Thankfully they decided not to do it. I did not have the knowledge nor background to safely pull it off. I was lucky in many ways that my stupidity did not get in my way.

I also played the surprise villain that was mentioned throughout the movie. Queenie. At the end (spoiler alert) She jumps out of the bushes. Trampoline. Long cold night. I was not originally supposed to play Queenie. The actress that was booked ended up not showing up. Lucky her. The make-up process was long and exhausting. Took four hours to apply glue, rubber and hair. Since a stunt performer (me) would be playing the part, we decided to make it more dramatic than just coming out of the bushes. So, I used a trampoline and leapt OVER the bushes. Now, I understand that that is considered an iconic moment.

I had no idea that this movie would become such a cult classic down the road.

MOTHER'S DAY

I had a manager at the time. He also took control of my stunt career. They were meant to be side jobs in-between acting gigs. He put together my first stunt composite. This is usually a headshot with stunt pictures on the reverse side. Only problem was that none of the stunt pictures were me. They were from movies I hadn't worked on. Sadly, I did not know better. Once I figured it out, I changed my composite to a more accurate view of what I actually did and not what I thought I could do. I wish I still had a copy of that one, but I will show you some of the newer ones I did to replace the fake one.

Scott Leva
SAG / AFTRA / AEA

L.A. – Teddy's – (213) 462-2301
N.Y. – Service – (212) 724-2800

Scott Leva

Height: 5' 10"   Hair: Brown
Weight: 165   Eyes: Blue
Suit: 40R   Pants: 30/33
Shirt: 15/33   Shoe: 10D

Scott
Leva

DGA / SAG
AFTRA / AEA

(213) 462-2301

79

"SPACE TRUCKERS" / DENNIS HOPPER

"LOIS & CLARK" /
DEAN CAIN

"ROBIN HOOD: MEN IN TIGHTS" / CARY ELWES

"LOIS & CLARK" / JOHN SHEA

"MOBSTERS" / CHRISTIAN SLATER

"WHITEMEN CAN'T JUMP" / WOODY HARELSON

SCOTT LEVA

SAG / AFTRA / AEA

(213) 462-2301
(213) 469-9980

CL inc.
talent agency

Scott Leva
843 No. Sycamore Avenue
Los Angeles, California 90038
(213) 461-3971

SCOTT LEVA
Height: 5' 10" / Weight: 165 lbs.
Hair: Brown / Eyes: Blue
Suit: 40R / Shirt: 15/33
Pants: 31/35 / Shoe: 10D

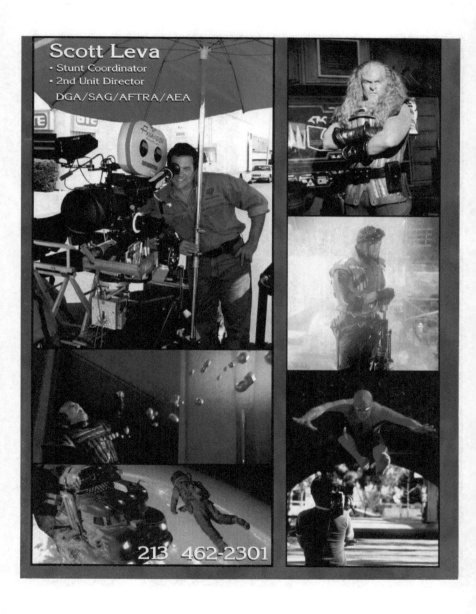

85

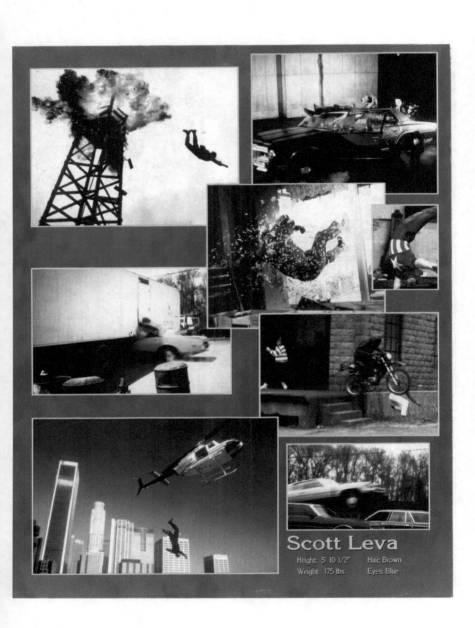

Scott Leva

Height: 5' 10 1/2"   Hair: Brown
Weight: 175 lbs   Eyes: Blue

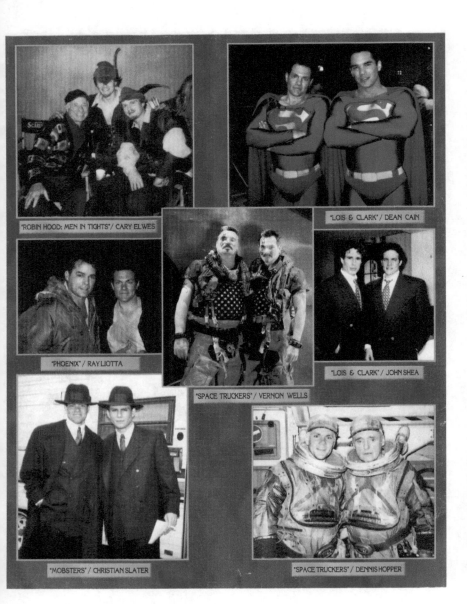

"ROBIN HOOD: MEN IN TIGHTS" / CARY ELWES

"LOIS & CLARK" / DEAN CAIN

"PHOENIX" / RAY LIOTTA

"SPACE TRUCKERS" / VERNON WELLS

"LOIS & CLARK" / JOHN SHEA

"MOBSTERS" / CHRISTIAN SLATER

"SPACE TRUCKERS" / DENNIS HOPPER

Stunt work is a serious business. It is not a part time job. You do not exaggerate about your skills or what you have done. It can be very dangerous. I was lucky to survive, and even luckier that my career did not end due to my false credits, ignorance, and outright stupidity.

There is a saying, "What doesn't kill you makes you stronger". I can attest to that. In my mind, in-between acting jobs (few and far between) I worked in stunts but it was really the other way around.

Early on I was cast in a traveling tour of *"Dames at Sea"*. Unlike college, I played the lead and had a very genuine relationship with my leading lady. I did other plays in the city, some of which, I would sometimes be the fight choreographer as well as act in it. Shakespeare mainly. I actually got some decent reviews for my choreography.

LINA MANNING (Mona) appeared recently in a national cereal commercial and has an extensive background in professional theater, including starring roles in California productions of "Oklahoma!," "The Apple Tree," "Guys And Dolls" and "The Man Who Came To Dinner."

SCOTT LEVA (Dick) has been seen in the movies "The Greek Tycoon" and "All The President's Men," and has been featured in theatrical productions of "Dark Of The Moon," "The Importance Of Being Earnest" and "Rally Round The Flag Boys." He also makes appearances throughout the country and on television as Spider Man.

LAUIE WINOGRAND (Ruby) studied acting at New York's Loft Theater, appeared in the "Magic Dragon Theatre" videotape for Todd Rundgren's Utopia Concert Tour and sang with the rock band Joe Cool.

Center Stage Presents The Musical Comedy

DAMES AT SEA

Book And Lyrics By George Haimsohn • Music By Jim Wise

Directed By Henry Edgar
Assisted By Carole Bennett

Produced By Carl Cole
Assisted By Barbara Powell

Choreography By Jim Snyder
Mr. Snyder's Services A Courtesy Of The Esperance Dance Theater

Musical Director — David Potts
Costumes By Cindy Lawrence

Technical Director — Bob Tremer
Scenic Design By Paul Brown ★ Lighting By Bob Tremer

Superintendent Of Transportation— Scott Cole

Cast Of Characters

Mona Kent	Lina Manning
Hennessey	Lawrence Baldwin
Joan	Bethann Tharpe
Ruby	Laurie Winogrand
Dick	Scott Leva
Lucky	Anthony Smith
Captain Courageous	Lawrence Baldwin

Musical Numbers

Act One— A Broadway Theater In The Early Thirties

Wall Street	Mona
It's You	Ruby And Dick
Broadway Baby	Dick
That Mister Man Of Mine	Mona
Choo Choo Honeymoon	Lucky and Joan
Sailor Of My Dreams	Ruby
Singapore Sue	Dick and Company
Good Times Are Here To Stay	Joan and Company

Act Two— Aboard The Battleship

Dames At Sea	The Company
The Beguine	Mona, Captain
Raining In My Heart	Ruby
There's Something About You	Dick, Ruby
Echo Waltz	Mona, Ruby, Joan
Star Tar	Ruby, Dick, Lucky, Hennessey
Let's Have A Simple Wedding	The Company

I took a break from stunts for a while when I decided to go to acting school. Now, I had taken classes on and off. With some very famous teachers I might add. Uta Hagen, Stella Adler, and Lee Strasberg. If I knew then what I know now, I might have taken it more seriously. I also was lucky enough to audit at the Actor's Studio. It is exactly what it sounds like. While auditing, I did not participate, I observed.

My father had an "in" at Julliard. I did not realize how prestigious a school it was then. I auditioned. Did a good job, but I was not willing to give four more years of my life to school, so I opted for what I call a Mini-Julliard. It is better known as "Circle in the Square". It had many of the same programs with the same teachers as Julliard, and it was only a two-year program.

During my time at Circle, I met a lot of good people. Some of the students, all of the teachers. We had dance, voice, singing, movement, technique, scene study, and stage combat courses. The stage combat teacher was a well know fight choreographer who did most of the fight choreography for Broadway. It was an amazing experience.

I also met my second serious girlfriend, Leslie. She was very popular with the guys at our school, everyone wanted to go out with her. We were scene partners and one thing led to another. I am not going into much detail out of respect for her.

I had a student loan to pay for the school, and had some money saved from earlier jobs. This was helpful as living in New York can be expensive, however Leslie and I moved in together, and that was helpful with expenses as well.

Having put most of my film and TV aspirations aside for a while gave me more time to take promotional gigs for Marvel.

AND this is where I became, "Spider-Man".

CHAPTER
Nine

DOES WHATEVER
A SPIDER CAN

Marvel became my second home. I spent a lot of time at those offices. Whenever I went to meet with the promotions department, I would drop in on the Marvel bullpen. I got to meet the creators and see what went into the stories and art. I met Stan Lee who spent limited time at the office, John Romita, Marie Severine, Al Milgrom, Tom DeFalco, Ralph Macchio. Denny O'Neil, Mark Gruenwald, Carl Potts. Archie Goodwin, Louise ("Weezie") Jones/ Simonson, her husband Walt, Danny Fingeroth (who I will be forever grateful), Eliot Brown and Jim Shooter who was a giant in both stature and creativity. These are just a few of the many creative forces in the Marvel Bullpen I was lucky enough to meet, associate with, and even work with. Early on, I would introduce myself. I think John Romita was the art director at that time. I got to meet with the Spider-Man editors. They were the first to take notice of my resemblance to Peter Parker. They were also impressed with my knowledge of the character and would listen to some of my insight into what I thought about the comics and where I hoped they would go. Once I became a regular visitor there, most of the people I met would introduce me to many of the other creators.

Playing Spider-Man was fun. I also got to play Captain America, (I used lifts) The Green Goblin, and The Thing. It was a large rubber molded costume that was very hot and very uncomfortable. There was a similar molded Hulk costume that thankfully I did not fulfill the size requirements.

I traveled a lot. I mean a lot. Everywhere in the United States that had a mall or toy store that wanted a Marvel character, we were there.

Now I should mention that I was not the first choice to do the more prestigious promotions. The promotion department had their favorite actor for that, I will call him Spidey 1. He was tall and lanky. He was muscular but more like The Electric Company's Spider-Man compared to the comic book version.

On the plus side, I was the favorite amongst the bullpen and creators. Any Marvel related event that dealt with having Spider-Man, I was their guy. That all stemmed from them getting to know me in a personal way, compared to a professional one. Also seeing me perform at comic conventions as Spidey as well as in the office when I would drop by made them see me as the real deal. I was the actual persona of our wall crawling hero to them. So, when a comic related event was being booked, they would request me from the promotions department.

I guess it was more flattering to be the favorite amongst creators, than the promotions department. Although I understand that I was their second favorite, I still got some pretty cool events.

When the Macy's Day Parade decide to include Spider-Man the first year, I was the one promotions felt was best due to my acrobatic abilities. I walked the entire parade route on the day. It was amazing (No pun intended). I did back flips, handsprings, walked on my hands. I was all over the place. I was initially surprised that they picked me over Spidey 1 for this gig, but they explained my acrobatics were a huge plus here.

The following year Marvel had a float in the Parade. We had a slew of Marvel characters on the float. Spider-Man (Spidey 1) of course, Spider-Woman, Hulk, Dr. Strange, the Enchantress, Wolverine, and I can't remember them all, but it was colorful. I was Daredevil. It was the year the balloon was first introduced.

Macy's Thanksgiving Day Parade

One of our most prestigious events was when Marvel was invited to the White House Easter Egg event when Jimmy Carter was president. Spidey 1 got the coveted Spider-Man spot. Promotions called in a few favors and got back a busy working actor who was

one of their original Captain Americas, Johnathan Frakes. Yes, Johnathan Frakes who was Captain Riker of Star Trek fame. (Side note: Later on, I ended up working on that show as well.) We had all of the costumed Marvel heroes in this event including Spider-Man, Captain America, Spider-Woman the Green Goblin, The Thing, and The Hulk. I played The Thing. A friend of mine, Ben, was The Hulk.

There were security measures. We had to have background checks. We had military personnel as our escorts during the event. Spidey 1 got into some minor trouble when he snuck up on the White House guard rail to pose without letting anyone know. Security ran up and was all over him. Kind of funny, but in the end not a big deal.

Ben and I had a schedule for performances due to the weight, and temperature of our molded costumes. A half hour on and a half hour off. We got pretty friendly with our military escorts. Mine was a Marine, Ben's was Navy. Typically, those two don't mix well.

That said, they wanted to try on the suits and go out for us. We were more than happy to oblige. Our guys in these heavy hot molded suits walked all over the place. They were out there for over an hour at a time. Nice for us, not so nice for them. Finally, my Marine started to head back but halfway back, he stopped in his tracks and in a loud bellowing voice yelled, "Hell NO! Marines don't come in before Navy."

He was out there for at least another twenty minutes before they both came in. He was completely drenched in sweat. We were a bit concerned that this would come back on us, but thankfully it did not, and we were actually commended for doing a fantastic job; above and beyond. If the ladies from promotions read this, they will most likely realize exactly what happened that day.

Our weekend and longer excursions were great. I loved the crowds. It's amazing to see kids when they see their heroes. We had a cool party favor that was a streamer which imitated what it looked like for Spider-Man to throw his Spidey-web. I held it in my hand, threw my hand, and a series of thin paper streamers would come out. I had a few of these. They were the white ones, not the multicolored ones. Once in a while, when kids would ask me to shoot a web, I threw the party streamer. They got so excited. Sometimes acrobatics would not be enough. I am not just an actor in a suit to these kids, I am Spider-Man.

Which brings me to an interesting story. "The Kid Who Collects Spider-Man". This was an actual story I was part of.

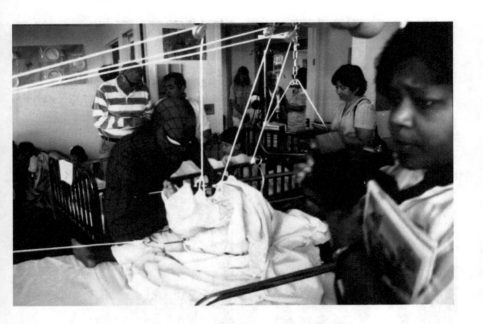

As part of our promotional meet and greets, we would visit children's hospitals. I would jump around and do my Spidey antics. I was asked if I would visit the Cancer ward. Of course. There was one room in particular that I was told I must visit. Now, sadly I do not remember the child's name. I am pretty sure it was not Tim Harrison like the boys in Spider-Man # 248, but just for story-sake we will call him Tim.

He was an avid Spider-Man fan. Comics, View Master, coloring books, posters, you name it, he had it. He probably knew more about Spidey than I did. And that's saying a lot.

When I first came into his room, his mother was sitting next to him. "Look who's here to see you."

Tim thought I was just another doctor dressed up to give him an injection or something else medical. He was not buying it.

So, he decided to ask me comic-related questions.

"What were Peter's real parents name?"

"Richard and Mary Parker."

"What was the name of the wrestler Spidey wrestled in his first appearance?"

"Crusher Hogan."

And so on, and so on.

He was impressed, but not completely sold.

"Do something only Spidey could do."

I told him I could not use my web shooters in the hospital due to sanitary concerns. Maybe I should just leave… I turned, ran up the wall, did a back flip with a half twist and landed in a classic Spidey pose.

"Mom! Did you see that? Did you see what Spidey did?"

As far as he was concerned, I was the real deal.

We spent the next half hour talking Spider-Man. He was embarrassed about being bald due to treatments. I rubbed his head. "You look just like me," I said as I rubbed the top of my masked head.

This kid was an avid fan. He knew everything Spider-Man. Before I was going to leave, he asked me to remove my mask. I said I couldn't. He said he already knew that I was Peter Parker. I hesitated, but what the heck, I unzipped the suit and unmasked. Thankfully, I had an uncanny resemblance to our favorite wallcrawler's real identity.

He was so ecstatic. I was real. I was Spider-Man / Peter Parker. As I left, his mother followed me into the hall and gave me a big tearful hug. This was the best medicine her son could get.

I do not know what happened to Tim. He was pretty badly off. I am just glad to have made a very difficult time for him a bit easier.

The comic story #248, "The Kid Who Collects Spider-Man" by Roger Stern regarding Spider-Man visiting a boy with Leukemia is considered one of the top ten Spider-Man stories of all time. I get it. I lived it.

CHAPTER
Ten

WORKIN' 9 TO 5

Marvel Promotions had an idea they wanted to test out. They wanted to have Spider-Man at the Marvel Offices at Park Avenue South in New York and when a client needed something delivered, they would have Spider-Man do the delivery. I was the initial test pilot. I had a small office space, with a desk and a phone where I usually read plays or books until I would get the call to take a delivery to a client. We would call for a taxi, so I could take the taxi to the client. Marvel had not set up any particular means of transportation at that time. When I arrived at the client, they would usually get excited by seeing Spider-Man deliver whatever it was that Marvel had sent. I would then return to the streetside and flag a taxi to return me to the Marvel offices. This worked out ok. Now, New York taxis are infamous. It was not always easy to get one, particularly during busy hours, or worst case, rainy days.

On one specific day, it was overcast. I got a delivery, suited up, and got a cab to take me the client's business. All went great, until I had to return. Now, it was pouring rain. I could not get a cab to save my life. Hard enough to flag down a cab dressed like Spider-Man, even harder in the rain. So, I did what any steadfast New Yorker would do; I took the subway.

There I was riding the subway, holding a handle in the subway car dressed as Spidey.

Yes, I got a few looks, but New York is famous for crazy situations, so I fit right in.

Once I got back and explained the issue with transportation, promotions decided to see what they could do to rectify it.

We found out that Marvel had an account with a limousine and a taxi service.

Problem solved.

Moving forward, anytime a delivery was made, we contacted the taxi service, and it was easy to get there and back. Sometimes during slower traffic, I rode on the roof of the taxi.

We changed it so I alternated weeks with Spidey 1. I would do one, he'd do the other. The days were good, pay was decent, and it enabled me to submit for acting roles.

One time during Valentine's day, Marvel Promotions called in an army of Spider-Men to deliver Valentine's gifts to the clients. It would have been too big a job for just me and Spidey 1. So, on that particular day there were six or seven of us. They brought in

Spider-Men of all shapes and sizes. As I mentioned earlier, Marvel Promotions had a group of actors that did promotions. Outside of group appearances, I never really got close with any of them. We all had our own take on how Spidey should be played. To most of them, it was a side job. To me? A dream job to play my all-time favorite hero.

When we delivered the valentines or packages, the clients would be ecstatic. Seeing a real live superhero gracing their office, made their day. Most of the time they would want to take pictures, some even wanted autographs for their kids. Of course, I would always do something Spidey style. Flips off tables. Leaping over chairs or even people. It was fun for me, and for them.

A perk of this gig was that they had a library of bound Marvel books. They had the original comics bound in a black cover with gold trim. The older rare books were missing, but I got to reread a lot of the old comics I had not visited in a while. My own comic collection was still in Maryland. I had most of the old issues, and various other comic publications as well. So, it was nice to be able to reread these again after so many years.

Side story, when I retrieved my comic collection from my home in Maryland, I also had the collection bound for easier access. This was before Marvel put out their Marvel Masterworks Series.

Now, getting to know the Marvel Bullpen was a plus. I got hands on experience with seeing how the stories and comics were created. During some of my many comic convention appearances with Marvel Bullpen members, I would get to be involved in some of the story ideas. It was fun. I felt like part of the team. One time during a plane flight to a comic convention, the editor, I believe it was Ann Nocenti, had asked for ideas on how Spidey could beat the unstoppable Juggernaut. We all had ideas. I remember saying to wrap him in a web cocoon. In the end Spidey fought him at a construction site, and Juggernaut was encased in cement. It was fun to throw out ideas though.

I also had a neat idea that I showed the editors for a Spider-Man cover. It showed Spider-Man in his regular blue and red costume, and his shadow on the wall was the black suit. They liked the concept, but it was not used.

As I mentioned earlier, Spidey 1 was the favorite in the promotions department. He tended to get some of the choice appearances and promotions.

I would say there was a friendly competition between us.

Once in a while, we would get to audition for various outside non promotional jobs. In some cases when asked, Marvel Promotions would give casting the names of prospective Spideys from their promotions roster. There was an audio book that neither Spidey 1 nor I booked, however another promotions actor got the gig.

The biggest one, was a national commercial for Atari Spider-Man video game. All the Marvel Spider-Men were submitted. At the initial audition I heard Pam with Marvel Promotions department really pushing for Spidey 1. Thankfully, it ended up to be a non-Marvel choice. It was a professional commercial so casting was looking at actors from everywhere including agent submissions, and of course Marvel itself. My commercial agent negotiated the deal for me.

At the audition, we were asked about our background with Spider-Man. One of our Marvel performers pulled out his suit from his bag and said, "I am Spider-Man!" He did not put on the suit.

During my audition, I also pulled out the suit, but proceeded to put it on, and BAM! I became Spider-Man; moving, flipping, being sarcastic. They asked me to wait around and read with some of the actors auditioning for The Green Goblin part.

I do not know what Spidey 1 did at his audition, but I can attest to the fact that Spidey 1 was a very talented actor, and that even though how we presented Spider-Man would be different, he was a strong performer. I think I just had more of a bond with Spidey in that moment. Needless to say, I got the part. I was cast over Marvel and non-Marvel actors. A non-Marvel performer got the part of The Goblin.

It was a fun, exciting commercial shoot. The Goblin's mask had animatronics that made the eyes move and blink.

The action was right out of the comic book. They used a teeter board to propel the Goblin up onto the wall as I was playing the game.

Marvel Promotions and a few Marvel executives were there as well.

During that time, National Commercial Spots paid a small fortune for the commercial. I was able to live very comfortably for a while off that particular commercial.

CHAPTER
Eleven

COVER "BOY" MODEL

Among acting classes, auditions, and various other things, I kept pretty busy. Spider-Man became a side gig that helped me meet people in the film industry and that became a great help down the road.

As I said earlier, I was the real Spider-Man as far as the Marvel Bullpen was concerned.

I did a comic photo cover which is probably what I am best known for to this day; "The Amazing Spider-Man #262".

Bob Layton, the famous comic book artist, writer, editor, and designer, had done a comic story for Spider-Man labeled a "Special Issue", but I believe it was done as the actual replacement issue incase the planned issue did not make the deadline for publication. Bob had also done a cover in case this one did not work. Thankfully the photo cover did work.

Eliot Brown oversaw making this now classic cover. Eliot is one of the most genuine and nicest people I have ever had the pleasure of dealing with. We set up at Marvel in the "proof" room in what seemed like a utility closet. The proof room held all the proofs that were sent to the editors before approval and publication. Quite a few shelves were there with what seemed like endless rolls of proofs.

Eliot himself was in the photo as the photographer. He is actually holding a tape dispenser with a flash on it and a remote button to shoot the actual picture. I don't remember how long it took to get this shot, but it was fun.

Below are some photos that were not used from that shoot.

©Eliot R. Brown

The Actual Photo Used for the Cover

One of the coolest things was, even though the Marvel creative staff saw me as Spider-Man, many of them felt I was so close to Peter Parker, that I could pull off this cover. That was a huge selling point for me further down the road.

During my time at Marvel, I was involved with lots of cool projects. One I did was known as a fummetti. It is a photo style comic that was on the inside front and back cover. I had some fun with that as well. It was published in Ka-Zar.

In the credits it gave the actors as "SCOTT LEVA AND A RUTHLESS GANG OF INCORRIGIBLE STREET TOUGHS."

Those street toughs were all Marvel writers, editors, and artist. Script was by Danny Fingeroth who, down the road, brought me in for another one of a kind photo cover shoot. And, Vince Colletta was the photographer. Quite a list of who's, who.

... WORK YOU DO BETTER THAN ANYONE...

(... EXCEPT MAYBE WOLVERINE.)

WHUNK

SURE, IT'S GRITTY WORK... THIRSTY WORK...

KA-BONK!

AND WHEN IT'S OVER, YOU LIKE TO RELAX AS HARD AS YOU WORK. AND YOU SHOULD. YOU DESERVE TO. THAT'S WHY NOW... NOW IT'S...

...KA-ZAR TIME.

♪ WHEN IT'S TIME TO RELAX... ONE MAG STANDS CLEAR... IF YOU'VE GOT THE TIME... WE'VE GOT THE KA-ZAR...♪

KA-ZAR, THE CHAMPAGNE OF PRINTED COMICS.

Script: **DANNY FINGEROTH**   Photography: **VINCE COLLETTA**   Lettering: **RICK PARKER**
Actors: **SCOTT LEVA & A RUTHLESS GANG OF INCORRIGIBLE STREET TOUGHS**

121

Now, I was very involved with stunt work at the time. I was actually making a decent living as a stunt man. I was working with some of the top stunt people in the industry, both from New York and California.

The grandfather of New York stunt work was a stuntman named Alex Stevens. I mentioned Alex earlier when I was on Superman the Movie. I was getting more and more work on film and TV shows.

At the time, there were three competing stunt associations in New York. The main two were The East Coast Stuntmen's Association and Stunts Specialists. The East Coast Stuntmen's Association was founded by Alex, and Stunt Specialists was founded by Victor Magnotta. They were the top dogs in town.

Alex was the guiding force behind New York's stunt community working on films. In most cases, the films that came from Los Angeles (Hollywood) hired stunt coordinators who came out of Hollywood, and they gave their top spots to their team or group members. New York stunt men only got tiny scraps of work from Los Angeles-based studios.

Alex had actually put together a picket line with other East Coast stuntmen and interrupted a film shoot conducted by a Los Angeles studio. I understand that after that, things changed.

Before really getting fully into stunts, I was working at a local gymnastics studio on Sutton's Place. It was called Sutton's Gym. A lot of the working stunt people came there to train, and I made friends and contacts. I had already met Alex, so that was a bit of an in.

During my time in New York, I had already worked on quite a few films and TV show.

"Superman", "Prizzi's Honor", "Fort Apache the Bronx", "The World According to Garp", "Splash", "The Cotton Club" and "Over the Brooklyn Bridge". Vic Magnotta was the main stunt coordinator I worked with. He tended to get most of the main movies. I worked for Vic through other stunt people I got to know and befriend such as Jerry Hewitt, Edgard Mourino and Tom Wright. Tom later became a very successful actor. He played George's boss, Morgan, on "Seinfeld". Most recently he played a pivotal role on "Daisy Jones & The Six".

Not sure he remembers me, but some of his advice while we were on set was instrumental in helping me grow as a stunt performer.

While working on "Splash" we would be waiting for what felt like forever for our shot (Hurry up and wait is a common term in our industry). This would give us time to hang out and chat for a while.

I remember while working on "The World According Garp" (one of my favorite books) that some of us were asked to fill seats in the movie theatre scene. This was cool. I got to hang with the director, George Roy Hill, (huge fan) and talk about planes (he was a bi-plane fanatic) and of course, movies in general.

It was my understanding that Mr. Hill gave Robin Williams specific instructions. "No adlibbing." During one take, Robin came into the theatre looking for his wife, one of the patrons said, "quiet", and Robin adlibbed, "fuck you." Mr. Hill, yelled, "Cut. Back to one. ROBIN? No adlibs."

That was cool.

I worked on a few TV shows like "Saturday Night Live", "The New Mike Hammer", and "The New Show". I was the stunt coordinator on that one, and happily repaid many of my stunt comrades that helped me along the way.

I also took some jobs as a stunt coordinator on some low budget films, mainly horror. "The House on Sorority Row", and probably one of the most famous, that people still talk to me about, "The Toxic Avenger".

That was where I met and had a special long-term relationship with Troma Films, specifically Lloyd Kaufman. Lloyd wrote the book, "All I Need To Know About FILMMAKING I Learned From THE TOXIC AVENGER: The Shocking True Story of Troma Studios".

In this book he basically tore apart his stunt coordinators. But not me. He was very generous with his praise.

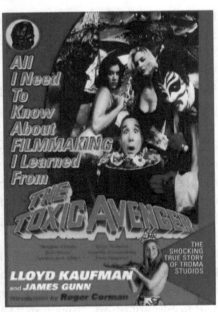

Lloyd was always asking me to come back and work on another film for him. We often met up at the San Diego Comic Convention. One time Lloyd was persistent in wanting me to at least set up a fire burn and high fall for their next installment of "Class of Nuke-'em High". I agreed, made a deal, and later that year they flew me out to New Jersey for one week of work. Lloyd had set up an assistant to work with me. He was not too thrilled with the prospect of working with another of Lloyd's friends. The last time they tried to do a fire burn, it did not go so well. They felt it would have been better if they put a lighter close up to camera.

So, my assistant talked to me about setting up the burn. "We need something BIG. Exciting. Needs to really stand out."

"Did you ever see the original Toxic Avenger movie? We want something close to that."

I answered, "As a matter of fact, I did. I was the stunt coordinator on that film."

"YOU WERE?"

His attitude towards me changed. I suddenly became somewhat of a celebrity. They even did interviews to include behind the scenes for upcoming re-releases of some of the Troma Films I worked on.

The fire stunt went off with-out a hitch.

I am somewhat responsible for Troma making "Toxic Avenger 4". Apologies to anyone that might be offended by that. When seeing Lloyd Kaufman at a convention, he was talking about a big studio wanting to do a Toxic Avenger reboot. It had been on hold for a while. I suggested he make another one while waiting. He jumped on that and moved very quickly. He wanted me to return as the stunt coordinator, but I was already set to work on the big X-Men film for 20th Century Fox.

Troma had a lot of A list talent associated with them before they were known. James Gunn, Vincent D'Onofrio, Trey Parker, Samuel L. Jackson, Marisa Tomei, and Carmen Electra, to name a few. I am in good company to say the least.

Another film that I was stunt coordinator on was "Desperately Seeking Susan" which had starred Rosanna Arquette and Madonna. Truthfully, I had no idea who she was. I was referred for the job by an actor, Aiden Quinn, who I was training for a Broadway production of "Cowboy Mouth". My girlfriend, Leslie, was a spot-on double for Rosanna. There were very few stunts, but it was a learning experience. I have a lot of respect and admiration for Susan Siedelman, the director.

An interesting coincidence happened while we were shooting a sequence near the Statue of Liberty. One of the extras was the stuntman, Eric Pederson, who worked with us at Montgomery College. Small world.

Now what does any of this have to do with Spider-Man or moving to California you might ask?

I was living with my girlfriend, Leslie, at the time. She was the girl I met at Circle In The Square theatre school. She started working as a stunt woman through me.

I was supposed to double the lead kid on, "First Born" the movie. One of the stunt doubles got severely injured, and Vic, the stunt coordinator was replaced by Glenn Wilder. A true stunt legend who would fill a book and then some with his history. Another stunt legend, Dar Robinson, was in town preparing a movie and worked with Glenn, doubling Peter Weller. My girlfriend doubled Terri Garr. Long story short, we got to be friends with Dar and his wife Linda.

I worked on "Turk 182". Dar was the stunt coordinator. We would hang out and talk between shoots.

Dar was most famous for holding the world record for highest high fall, 311 feet. Another stuntman was in direct competition with him, and they kept upping the ante. In the end, the other stunt man, A.J. Bakunus, died while trying to beat that record.

While working with Dar, he got word that another stuntman had just beat his record. Dan Koko.

I could see his wheels turning. "You're going to beat that aren't you," I asked.

"I'm going to make it unbeatable," he answered. "I'm going to do a mile. Under controlled conditions, you already hit maximum velocity. With the right layered air bag, and the proper jump suit. It can be done."

I had no doubt he could do it.

He would also keep giving me the "Go West Young Man" speech. It was one of the motivating factors that helped me decide to move. My girlfriend had family there so that helped as well.

So, we decided we would move to sunny California.

CHAPTER
Twelve

CALIFORNIA, HERE I COME

Before leaving for California, I was still working with Marvel. I was told that they would be happy to set up appearances through their Los Angeles office. That was very helpful.

Now Marvel had decided to do some radical changes with some of their flag ship comics. Spider-Man, for the first time, was getting a new costume that was a symbiote that he obtained during the Marvel Superheroes Secret Wars, originally conceived by Jim Shooter.

Marvel Promotions was asked to whip up the Black Spidey suit to debut at a huge ComicCon. I was chosen as the model and the suit was fitted to me.

I, along with the Marvel Elite, attended the convention. Jim Shooter, Ron Frenz (the current Spider-Man artist), Roger Stern, and Stan The Man himself.

They were supposed to roast Spider-Man.

Nothing was really prepared. So, we met in a side room, and they decided that Spidey would roast them. Thanks for throwing me under the bus.

Marvel had just published a "Spider-Man: National Committee for Prevention of Child Abuse" special comic at that time. It was an admirable undertaking. Very important.

So, I started off the "roast" by complimenting Marvel on their campaign against child abuse. After which I said, "Not many of you know this, but Jim Shooter has been accused of child abuse."

The room went silent. Jim looked shocked.

Then I said, "Who here has read Marvel Superheroes Secret Wars?"

Big laugh, from Jim as well, who also seemed a bit relieved.

I forget the other remarks I made about the other creators, but Stan?

I said, "What can I say about Stan Lee, that Stan hasn't already said about himself?"

Big laugh. Even from Stan.

I then went on to say (still performing as Spider-Man), "Stan called me into his office to fill me in on the new suit." Then in my best Stan Lee voice (I can do a spot-on Stan), "Spidey, you'll love it. Don't worry, it'll grow on you." (Reference to the symbiote.)
Stan retorted, "I don't sound like that!" Which of course he did.

Even bigger laugh.

We bantered back and forth, and there was an open Q & A from the audience. One question, (which we were hoping for) was, "Where is the new suit?"

Standing up, I forget who, one of the creators unzipped the back of the classic Spider-Man red and blue to reveal the new black symbiote suit.

The crowd went wild.

The rest of the convention was spent meeting and greeting. A few interviews, a few panels. One of which I jumped from a balcony to a flagpole, slid down, and then leapt on the stage. Even a fight with the Green Goblin.

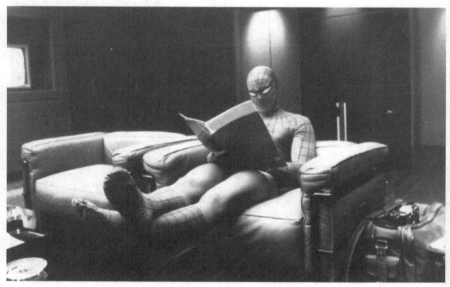

I was on a panel with Ron Frenz as well. That was so much fun. People treated me as Spider-Man. I was Spider-Man. Really liked Ron. Good artist, great guy. Even though it is only on Facebook, Ron and I are still friends. I remember how impressed he was with my knowledge of Spidey and he even commented to the audience there about my stature and the way I moved. THAT is what Spider-Man is.

Ron & Me on a Panel

A little while later I moved to California with my girlfriend Leslie. It was a disaster waiting to happen.

CHAPTER
Thirteen

LIFE OF A HOLLYWOOD STUNTMAN PART 1

Once we moved to California, we moved in with my girlfriend's mother. Not an ideal situation.

Her mother was very sweet. We pushed hard at the acting gigs. Got agents. The whole thing.

Getting stunt work was impossible. Even after meeting so many Los Angeles based stunt people while working in New York, I was still the new kid when I came to Los Angeles. Even with my credits, I was starting over.

I got a commercial agent. That helped. I booked a few. So did my girlfriend.

Leslie's mother, who was divorced, met a new man. They got married. He lived in Orange County. We ended up living in his house. It was nice, but the drive to and from Los Angeles was brutal.

I had called Dar Robinson, who was happy to hear from me. A bit busy, but once in a while I would be invited to his house in North Hollywood. I checked out his cool stunt toys and jumped on his trampoline.

Dar was an inspiration to me. He made me realize that stunts were more than just physical action. There was a science to making difficult stunts work. Calculations, testing. He was the main reason I started learning more about stunt equipment, how it worked, and eventually even improve upon it.

He told me how difficult it was to work as both a stuntman and an actor. It would be one or the other. Dar had always wanted to be an actor and was trying to move more in that direction. In Burt Reynolds movie, "Stick", Dar played "Moke", the Albino villain. He did an amazing first-time stunt on an apparatus he co-invented with Ky Michaelson. The Decelerator. What made it an amazing stunt was he fell backwards from the balcony shooting his gun with nothing but street below him.

Even with a friendship with Dar, stunt work was difficult.

While living in Orange County, I was awakened by the radio, "World famous stuntman Dar Robinson was killed in a movie stunt accident today". I was in shock. I always thought Dar was invincible.

And so, this was another time in my life when I decided to put stunts aside. I think the reality of life or death really hit me. If Dar Robinson, who I thought was invincible, could get killed doing a stunt, then what was I thinking? Was this where I really wanted to be? Also, Leslie was pushing me more towards acting. Interestingly enough, I got hired by Knotts Berry Farm to work in their stunt show. Stunts were and always will be in my blood. Not my dream job, but it was fun being able to act again in a live show.

Leslie got hired to work in the Knott's Berry Farm Calico Saloon. We went to work together.

Quite a few big-name stunt people worked at Knott's before they became working stunt people in the industry. Some very famous. A few I became friends with.

got more injuries working at Knotts than all the stunt work I did for TV and movies combined.

was seriously injured there while performing the high fall finale. The crash mat was old, and the middle was sagging. On this particular day, I bottomed out. This is something that happens when the safety mattress doesn't fully catch the performer and they feel solid ground on impact. It took me a few minutes to stand, but I was dizzy and in major pain. My back and neck were stiff and difficult to move. Don't remember what exactly happened afterwards. I was very disoriented. Paramedics came and looked after me backstage, and I was taken to a hospital.

I do not remember how long I was incapacitated. I was on workmen's comp disability for a while.

My relationship with Leslie got more strained. Between my injuries and her just wanting something else, we eventually split. She had gone back to New York to work as a stunt double on a film starring Tom Berenger. The first assistant director took a big liking to her. The stunt actress Patricia (who worked a lot as an actress) that was originally slated to play a speaking role was delayed, so the assistant director pushed Leslie into the role.

This pissed off a lot of the local stunt people. Leslie ended up in a relationship with the assistant director, and the rest was history.

In fairness, I was not the best boyfriend. I was self-indulgent and had a few indiscretions of my own. One with an incredible girl from Switzerland who I was head over heels for. Sadly, I messed that up and hurt this girl very badly.

Leslie and I would have most likely split up earlier, except she had a close relationship with my mother that made it difficult. My whole family really liked her.

It was a bad break up. Almost like a divorce. She took a lot of the things that we had together.

I moved to North Hollywood. I was still involved with Marvel appearances. They had set up a west coast office. Stan Lee was there as well. I worked with Stan a lot in the past, but we had never actually met outside of me being Spidey. That would soon change.

CHAPTER
Fourteen

SPIDER-MAN RETURNS

I made myself fully available for Marvel appearances. In between auditions and commercial work, it was my second job. I travelled a lot. My friend, Ben, had moved to California. We got together and tried to work on special events outside of Marvel. Ben was also still doing Marvel appearances.

I had developed an action show through Marvel that was pretty decent. "Spider-Man VS the Green Goblin". There were acrobatics, flash bombs, and even a sword fight. Marvel actually booked that show as an appearance quite a bit.

I did a lot of mall, toy fair, and trade show appearances. One in particular had booked both Ben and me at the San Diego Zoo. Marvel had booked a Spider-Man (Spidey 1) and Captain America for two weeks. We were to split the event. The first pair of performers would take the first week, me and Ben the second.

When I arrived at the San Diego Airport, the woman who picked me up was also the main sponsor and the person we reported to. She was a short heavy-set woman. She was very upset when we met and definitely not happy to see me.

When we got to the hotel that the Zoo had provided, I checked in, went to my room, and decided to visit Spidey 1. When I came into his room, the sponsor was sitting on his bed, looking very hurt. She got up and left.

It was obvious what was going on. Spidey 1 was sleeping with the sponsor. He let me in on what was going on. She was very attached to him. He said he tried to keep her at a distance, by being somewhat rude with her. He would not allow her to spend the night. He kept their dalliances strictly physical. But, having an intimate relationship with someone can cause a close attachment from one of the people involved. And, that is what happened. I expressed my concern. He said not to worry about it. It would all be fine. He insisted and said, "Please do not let the ladies at Marvel Promotions know anything about this."

Now, during my long career as Spider-Man, I had what would be considered hook-ups. Most of us did. I always kept them discreet and above board. No promises, no commitment. NO sponsors.

I did the appearance with Ben. Did my usual antics, acrobatics, and so forth. The sponsor just treated me with complete disdain.

I filled Ben in on the situation. "Oh, that makes sense. I wondered what her problem was."

Finished the event, flew home.

The following week I got a disturbing call from Barbara at Marvel Promotions. The sponsor was very unhappy with me. She said I had a lack of enthusiasm and was flirting while not paying attention to the kids. She said I had been extremely unprofessional.

None of that was true.

The sponsor was mad at Spidey 1, not me, but it didn't stop her from taking it out on me.

I was put on hold from appearances for Marvel until they could figure this out. I said she was completely off. I kept my word to Spidey 1 and did not tell Marvel Promotions about the actual event that led up to our sponsors dislike of me.

For the first time, I was no longer on the Marvel Promotions list.

About three weeks later I got a call from Barbara. I was back on and being sent on a promotion. What happened? "Everything was fine." She said they had gotten another side to what was happening at that time.

I found out that when they questioned Ben about my poor actions, he filled them in on the whole story. Spidey 1's relationship with the sponsor. Everything. Said I was perfect at the promotion and everyone except the sponsor loved me.

Thank you, Ben. I kept my word. This did not come from me.

I understand that Spidey 1 got a slap on the wrist.

I started doing fewer appearances. More so, because I was losing interest.

I was booked on an appearance at a licensing event, where all the big companies that license characters for products show off their products. I was with a main sponsor. I was asked to visit other sponsors as well. A few celebrities were there. Two that were favorites of mine: Mary Tyler Moore and Jon Voight. I got both of their autographs. I am sure I still have them somewhere.

Many of the other Marvel licensees were very unhappy with Marvel. They would tell me their issues with the company. Not my place, but I would listen. The main problem was the actual products. They looked cheap. Poor representation of the characters. That was partly on Marvel for not having quality control. Disney is famous for quality control. Their licensed products were perfect representations of the Disney brand.

Another convention I went to, one of my last Marvel appearances outside of California, was for videos and video games. A company had secured the rights to the Marvel 2099 characters in an exciting action RPG style game.

They had me dress up as Spider-Man 2099 at their booth. Biggest problem was they had the suit made without any measurements. It was a spot-on Spider-Man 2099 but seemed to have been fitted more for an Arnold Schwarzenegger body type. It fully bagged on me and was awkward and uncomfortable to wear. But I held out for the entire week. Truthfully? I don't think any of the attendees knew who Spider-Man 2099 was. In the end, the game was never released.

During my free time walking around I ran into my old acquaintance, Spidey 1. We exchanged pleasantries. The event with the San Diego Zoo and my almost getting fired came up. He was upset I told Marvel. He got in some hot water because of that. Not almost fired like me, but still. I explained that I said nothing, and that Ben relayed the story.

Hey, I like the guy. It is what it is. Or was what it was.

Meanwhile, I was squeaking by on a few acting roles. Commercials were paying decent royalties. I decided to keep most of my Marvel appearance work, close to home. I did a nice event with Golden Apple Comics and Children's Hospital. Became very good friends with the owner, Bill Liebowitz.

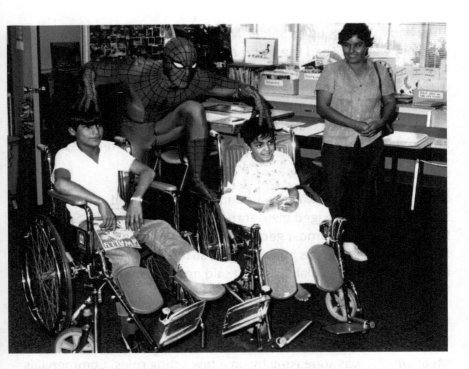

Made a few appearances at his store and helped with his awards venue, The Golden Apple Awards. It was there I met Jack Kirby and his wife, Rose. Jack thought I was the perfect Spider-Man. Exactly what he envisioned when he created Spider-Man. I was a bit confused by that, until I learned later about his feud with Stan about creative rights.

Jack (King) Kirby

Brinke Stevens

I met quite a few comic book creators there. Dave Stevens, (The Rocketeer), Kevin Eastman (Teenage Mutant Ninja Turtles) who was married to Julie Strain. Both of these creators I worked with in one capacity or another further down the road. I worked with a slew of Marvel and DC creators as well. Some of whom I already knew. Comics were still a bit of a passion for me. That would change.

CHAPTER
Fifteen

SPIDER-MAN: THE MOVIE

The concept of a Spider-Man movie was being shopped around for as long as could remember. I was a working stuntman in New York when I first heard that Roger Corman had acquired the rights. He was developing it for Orion Pictures.

I created a presentational package that I never sent to him as the film ended up in limbo. I think budgetary concerns were the main issue. I understand that Stan Lee had written the screenplay.

I was basically surviving as an actor in Los Angeles. My agent was William Felber. I liked him. He was a good agent, decent man.

Around 1985, Cannon Films headed by Menahem Golan and Yoram Globus had taken over the rights. They were famous for preselling films before they were made. That being said, I started doing my homework. I wanted in on this project no matter what.

Ads came out, and I started to see where and what I needed to be and do to get in on it.

I made some phone calls to Cannon. This got me in touch with casting, who in turn got me in touch with the publicity department. After a few meetings I was hired to do publicity photos for their ad campaign.

I learned that Tobe Hooper of "The Texas Chainsaw Massacre" fame was slated to direct it.

I found out everything I could regarding Mr. Hooper. I watched all his films, read whatever articles I could find. You name it.

Then I heard that he was going to be doing a remake of the classic, "Invaders from Mars". With my agent's help and my relationship with casting, I auditioned for and got a part. Marine #1. I had lines and everything. This brought me one step closer to getting in on the upcoming Spider-Man movie.

The night of the shoot, it was cold, it was late. We were behind schedule and the assistant director informed me we would not get to my scene. I said, "I was hoping to meet Tobe since he was involved with the Spider-Man film."

"Oh, he's not doing that anymore."

What?

I found out Joe Zito was the new director. Joe was the golden boy at Cannon. He did a low budget Chuck Norris film that was the highest grossing film for Cannon called, "Missing In Action".

From what I understood he ran into Menahem in the elevator at Cannon and mentioned wanting to do Spider-Man, but heard that Tobe was already attached. No problem. "You want Spider-Man? You got Spider-Man."

The film got fast tracked. The pictures I had taken for promotions were now in *Variety* and the *Hollywood Reporter*.
I got my agent to call. Nothing.

I still had a relationship with Marvel Promotions. Got a call. Stan Lee was doing a commercial spot for organ donor cards. He needed Captain America, The Hulk, and Spider-Man. "You interested?"

"Hell yes!"

I went to Marvel West, Stan's office. Suited up and we did the shoot. Ben was Captain America. I had met and worked with Stan quite a bit in the past. Never met him out of costume. He was impressed with the way I moved.

After the shoot, I put on my civvies and went into his office to say goodbye. (All planned.)

Introduced myself.

"Hey. You look just like Peter Parker!" (You don't say.)

"You know they're doing a movie." I heard something about it...

"You should try for it. You would be perfect."

Step one. Meet Stan the Man himself face-to-face. Not just as Spider-Man.

That became the beginning of a beautiful friendship. We talked almost weekly. I would stop by a couple times a month. Stan had some serious back issues. Even shaving could cause his back to go out. I was a bit of a fitness aficionado. I had worked with private trainers to get into fighting Spidey shape a long time ago. I gave Stan a workout program to help with his back pains. It worked. He had major relief. He would thank me for quite a while.

During this time, I was also doing various promos. Mainly associated with Marvel West and Stan. We worked the Equestrian Center. Stan wanted me to show him how to do my Spidey pose. He decided not to bend that low. We did a few conventions. It was fun.

He had put out a book called, "The Best of Spider-Man". Basically reprints of the daily newspaper comics. I had him sign a personalized copy.

All the while, I kept on top of The Spider-Man movie. I was going out of my way trying to get in to meet Joe Zito. My agent would call. They were told it was too early.

A sub agent named Michael Stroka (who was in the original "Dark Shadows" TV series and played the role of Alchetron) took over. He was all over it. I learned while writing this book that Michael passed away in 1998 from kidney cancer.

Still no luck. Cannon was releasing the promotional materials, and there was talk of me going to the Cannes Film Festival as Spider-Man.

The original poster had Tobe Hooper as the director.

I did promo pics as Peter Parker / Spider-Man. They are all over the internet. The Spider-Man leaping pictures used in the ads and promos were shot at a photo studio. I suggested using a trampoline to get the type of air borne action they were looking for. It worked perfectly. I was not thrilled with some of the pictures as there were better, more Spider-Man like poses. Not my call. Luckily, they gave me some copies.

I was putting another package together. Ron Frenz drew up a comic page for me that used my exact likeness as Peter Parker.

All my years at Marvel were paying off. Anyone who knew me was pushing for me to be in the film. Jim Shooter had written a script. He said he wrote it with me in mind for the role. As far as he was concerned, I was the perfect choice. You couldn't ask for a better support group than that.

By this time, Cannon Publicity, casting, and my agent were telling Joe Zito about me. Still too early.

One day, while I was visiting Stan, I asked if he would mind putting in a word for me to Joe about Spider-Man. Stan was pushing for the role of J. Jonah Jameson.

He said he would be happy to, but he wasn't sure what good it would do. "Who am I? Not sure they would listen to me."

I said, "Stan, you have a lot more pull than you think."

He did call. A few days later I got a call from my agent. Joe Zito wanted to meet me. "Who is this Scott Leva fellow everyone keeps telling me about?"

I got a meeting the next week.

I prepared for the meeting. I had my promotional packet ready to go.

We met at Cannon in his office. Talked a few pleasantries. At first, he was very professional. Business like.

"Tell me about Spider-Man," he said. Boy did he open a can of worms. I opened up full on about who Spider-Man / Peter Parker was. History, dysfunctions. Insecurities, strengths, weaknesses you name it.

Joe lit up. He was excited. Joe was a bit of a Spider-Man fan as well. We spent over an hour there. At the end, he mentioned his wife was doing a charity event at a nearby park that coming weekend. How would I feel about making an appearance as Spider-Man? I'd love to.

I called Marvel Promotions to give them a heads up. Told them it would be on me; would they be OK with it? They were fully on board.

I arrived at the park. Met Mrs. Zito. A really charming, sweet lady. She was excited to have me there.

I suited up. I had the full Spidey accessories and energy ready to go. I did a series of back handsprings with a layout, landing in a patented Spidey pose.

Grabbed a handful of the white party streamers, threw a bunch of webs at the kids. Moved around, joked around, had a ton of fun. I fully forgot why I was there and like any appearance or promotion, I just got into the moment.

Joe showed up. Watched a bit. We talked a while. I got back to finishing the party. I can't remember what the charity was for.

Afterwards, I changed. Joe and his wife thanked me. Joe said he would be in touch.

Things were going great.

I talked with Joe at least once a week. I was even invited to come by the office. I made sure to make a visit on his birthday with a special cupcake. His wife was there, and both were pleasantly surprised that I knew. I told him honestly, that I tend to research people I hope to work with.

Most of our talks were Spider-Man related. A lot of questions. I gave him insights into Peter Parker. How Spidey was an extension of him.

Joe started giving me story concepts. I found out the villain was going to be Dr. Octopus (He thought Bob Hoskins would be a good fit). He started asking about Doc Ock. I gave him a bunch of information, but I could do him one better.

I came back the next day with about five of my bound copies of Spider-Man comics. The introduction of Doc Ock in Spider-Man 3. Ocks return in 11 and 12. The master planner series with the famous Spidey story under the tonnage of wreckage from 33. A few more. Number 53. I bookmarked each comic. I said, this should give you a general idea of who this guy is. Take your time. No rush.

I got to hear story ideas. At one point, I was lucky enough to see some cool story boards. Scripts were written. None of them were what they should or could have been. They were missing the Spidey magic.

I remember Stan telling me what he thought. Yes, I was still hanging with Stan.

It seemed the script was the main issue.

In the meantime, the movie was interviewing crew members. Props, wardrobe, effects, and stunts. Joe met with Freddie Waugh. Fred was an avid Spider-Man fan. We knew each other from before. Fred was the stunt coordinator and pretty much Spider-Man for the Nicholas Hammond series.

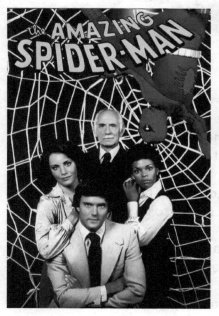

Fred told me that Joe asked about me during their interview and that Fred told him I would be a great choice. This was good news.

It looked as though the movie was going to happen. I was called by Cannon Publicity about working out details to go to Caanes.

Casting interviews were being set up. I was working with Michael Stroka at the time. He left William Felber and became my manager.

We worked hard on my audition. I had no problem with the Peter Parker dialogue. Spider-Man was a different issue. I was not as strong as I should be. I was not Spider-Man.

I finally said to Michael, "I need to wear the suit."

"What?"

"I can't be Spider-Man without the suit. I need the mask. So does Peter Parker. Spider-Man brings out the hidden side of Peter. Allows him to show his stronger more confidant side. Even in the comics, Pete needs some sort of mask to hide who he thinks he is, compared to who he is. He's worn a webbed stocking over his face, even a bag. He (I) needed the suit. Spider-Man is an extension of who Peter really is."

Michael was a bit confused, and slightly unsure. "Ok. Put on the suit. Let's see what happens."

I put on the suit. Boom! I am Spider-Man. The dialogue rolled off easily. I even added a bit of famous Spidey sarcasm to it.

Michael was stunned. "You're right. You need the suit. Let me call casting and see if they are ok with that."

They were.

On the day of the audition, I sat in a waiting room filled with about seven or eight other prospective Peter Parkers. One nervous actor started to talk to me. "Are you here for Spider-Man?"

"I am."

This is really cool." He introduced himself and started telling me more about himself. Michael grabbed my arm and took me into another room. "You need to get away from them," he said. "They can mess you up. Stay focused."

My turn was next. I headed into the nearest restroom and changed. I looked at myself in the Spidey suit. Full confidence. This is mine.

When I left the room the remaining actors all stared at me. They seemed a bit stunned.

I went into the audition room with Joe Zito and the casting directors. Joe laughed. "This is great! I love it! Let's see what you can do."

I perform the Spidey dialogue. No problem. Even did a little action and hit the poses.
Now for Peter. I unzipped the suit and took the mask off. No problem. I am Peter Parker.

They seemed pleased. Joe smiled from ear-to-ear.

I left feeling the best I ever had. It could not have gone better.

I heard later on that the other actor's agents had called and complained. They felt I had an unfair advantage wearing the suit. Casting said that the other actors were welcomed to that, I was the only one who thought of it.

Now prior to this casting session, names were being thrown around for the movie. Specifically, Spider-Man/ Peter Parker.

Tom Cruise, John Cusack, Michael Dudikoff (one of Cannon's big action stars), and Olympic Gold medalist Mitch Gaylord.

Early on, Joe had told me about a few of these choices. Michael Dudikoff was wrong for it as far as he was concerned. He screened the movie "American Anthem" starring Mitch Gaylord. Mitch was a nice guy, but not the right choice for this movie. All positive news for me.

I just had to sit and wait.

My appearance at the Caanes film festival was cancelled. Golan and Yorbas were going to be dealing with other projects.

The movie was still going, but they had some other deals they were focused on. I got a cool jacket though.

No big deal.

I went to the American Film Market that year. It was the week after my audition. The AFM is for distribution companies to set up meetings to try and sell their projects globally.

I tended to go every year to network.

I happened to run into Joe Zito there. Very happy to see me. He said, "You did a very good audition. I mean VERY good. That made my day."

Now the wait began. We heard news that Cannon had acquired the rights to "The Superman" franchise. Also, "He-Man, Masters of The Universe".

There was a mention that maybe Chris Reeve could play Spider-Man. Thankfully not a serious idea.

Cannon went full force on these two new sure-to-be-blockbuster movies.

And I waited.

I heard that the budget for Spider-Man had been cut. They were looking at studios in Italy.

And I waited.

Next I heard, more budget cuts. Still not happy with the script. I had some down time. So, with another comic fanatic fan friend of mine, Steve Webb, (yes, that's his real name) we took a run at our own Spider-Man script. We went back to the basics. We made Spider-Man and Doctor Octopus' origin mesh together.

Dr. Octavius had a huge insect phobia. During a class lecture in thermonuclear physics, da spider slowly moves down on a thin web in front of Ock. He went crazy. Swatted at it with his real arms and his waldo mechanical ones. There was a minor flash explosion. Everyone, including Peter ran to see if he was ok. The spider bit Peter, the mechanical arms were welded to Ock, and the story unfolded.

I gave the script to Joe Zito. He liked it, but the movie was on the back burner. He would most likely be doing another, "Missing in Action" film.

Now I had to get serious.

I had no idea when or even if this movie would be made.

I got a call from a talent agent, Sid Craig. He wanted a meeting. I was in the market for a new agent. Michael Stroka was still my manager.

Great. We set it up. We met. Small talk. Asked me to do a monologue. I did one from the play "Streamers". This same monologue got me an in with the casting director, Gary Schaffer who cast "Dynasty". He said it was one of his favorite plays and that he had never seen it performed better. I actually got a small part on "Dynasty" because of that.

Playing "The Waiter" on Dynasty

Sid was not as impressed. He said it was OK. Then he started talking about "The Spider-Man" movie. What made me think I was going to get it? He had two clients that were in the Spidey running. Michael Dudikoff and Mitch Gaylord. He told me all he had to do was call up Menahem Golan and tell him about all of Mitch's accomplishments. Gold medals, special Israeli awards, a long list that went over my head. He told this to Menahem. Mitch was in. Ok? So? Then he asked me if I would be putting all this Spider-Man movie stuff away. I said I would for the time being while the movie was on hold. But once it was up and running... I was all over it. He did not like that. It seemed he brought me in not to represent me, but to try to get me off the list of prospective Spideys. I already knew that Menahem was aware of Mitch. I also knew where he stood with the role.

No loss. Moving on.

I literally put all my eggs into one basket. My finances were hurting. I made calls for auditions, promotions, anything. I called Fred Waugh looking for work. I think he saw me as more of an actor than a stunt man.

I was getting desperate.

CHAPTER
Sixteen

WHO YOU GONNA CALL?

I started taking side jobs. One job I got, in particular, was similar to Spider-Man appearances. A friend of mine, Peter Mosen was a huge Ghostbusters fan. On weekends he would perform "Ghostbusters" birthday parties.

He and his other partner who played Egon had a falling out, so Peter asked me if I would play Venkman.

Doing my best Bill Murray impression, I agreed. It was kind of cool as I had worked on the original "Ghostbusters" movie back in New York.

Peter knew as much about "Ghostbusters" as I did about Spider-Man. He also had an uncanny resemblance to Dan Akroyd. Peter was amazing. He could make fantastic realistic costumes. He made a red and blue Spider-Man suit and a Symbiote Black suit that rivaled Marvel Promotions one. (I borrowed it for a few convention appearances.) He even made a Batman and Conan one. His costumes were spot on professional.

His props were even more detailed. His Proton packs lit up. He had a huge blow up Stay Puff Marshmallow man suit that made an appearance at the end of the party that the birthday boy or girl would capture. His Ecto Mobile was as real as they came.

His goal was to work on the next "Ghostbusters" movie. And he did. As an extra that got slimed in a restaurant. It was almost as much fun as doing Spider-Man appearances.

Met a lot of celebrities. Christopher Guest, Jamie Lee Curtis, and Vanna White. Producers and directors as well.

CHAPTER
Seventeen

LIFE OF A HOLLYWOOD STUNTMAN PART 2

I also started teaching at a Gymnastics Olympica. I met more and more stunt people there. It was how I learned the art of hustling. Hustling is when a stunt performer goes to a TV or movie set and tries to meet the stunt coordinator. I'd bring my headshot and resume' and hope that they could use me in some capacity.

I started the rounds. I would find out where they were shooting and do the best I could to get there.

One top stunt coordinator was pretty decent. He let me hang out on the set. At one time he asked to use my cell phone.

I said, "Sure, why not." These were when mobile phones were very large. The usage rates were astronomical.

He was on my phone until the battery died. $700.00 bill.

When he handed me the phone back, he said, "what do I owe you'? Never mind. I'll give you a job."

That never happened.

Many years down the road I was working on a TV movie that he was on too. One of the stuntmen that knew the story said, "Hey, Scott give (won't say his name out of respect) your phone."

I said no way.

He was surprised.

I told him the story. I told him I lost my phone service until I could pay the bill.

He said, "Did I do that? Sorry. I'll give you a job to make up for it."

I replied, "I won't hold my breath."

I never did get a job from him.

It got more difficult.

As I mentioned earlier, my parents had bestowed certain values to us early on. One of which was I never saw "color". I hate when people make that comment, but in this case, it's true. As far as we were concerned, people were people no matter what color they were.

I usually hustled with another stunt person. We would go to sets and if one of us knew the stunt coordinator we would make an introduction. One time I was hustling with my friend Terry (who I later learned was heavy into drugs). We went to visit Universal Studio. We went to the backlot of the film "Ghostdad". As we neared the trailers, the director with some of his crew stepped out. The director was Sidney Poitier. I loved his work. Three of my favorite films are "Lilies of The Field", "A Patch of Blue" and of course "In the Heat of the Night".

I went over to them and said, "Excuse me. Do you know where we could find Alan Oliney?"

Mr. Poitier asked, "Who is that?"

I answered, "he is your stunt coordinator."

"Oh," he said. "He's on Stage 18."

I thanked him and as he left, I said, "Excuse me. I am a huge fan of yours. Your work has inspired me for years, I would love to shake your hand."

He seemed genuinely touched. We shook hands. As they left, Terry snickered and said, "So, you shook the n@%gers hand."

I was appalled. That was the last time I ever hustled with anyone again, and the last time I EVER dealt with Terry. He took a special moment, and tarnished it.

I got an offer to go back to New York and work for Troma again. They were set to do "Troma's War". It was a low budget movie, but who was I to turn down anything?

I went back to New York. I knew enough people that finding a place to stay was not an issue. Once we began to film, we had living facilities there.

Explosive High Fall

Directing the Action

Stunt Team on Troma's War

One of the things I liked about Troma was being able to create action. I would come up with exciting sequences that invariably made it into the movie. Sometimes I would make a joke, and Lloyd would do it. I suggested at the end of "Troma's War", that everyone in the final shot who were lying there dead, sit up and wave. And, so they did.

When I worked on the first, "Toxic Avenger" I was given the same liberties. I created high falls, fire stunts, car chases (even brought Alex Stevens in for that). I played the policeman who grabs Melvin (Toxie) after he fell into the toxic waste.

I thought it would look cool if my hands burst into flame. I came up with a sequence where Toxie met a bunch of thugs in an alleyway and took them out.

"What is Toxie doing there, why would he be there?"

"I don't know, he's taking a piss on the wall?"

"Perfect! Let's shoot it."

At the end of the fight, after pure mayhem, I had one guy left.

"What does he do?"

Again, "I don't know, he wets himself and runs away."

"Perfect! Let's shoot it!"

And on and on. I learned a lot from my previous no brainer attitude. I took safety and precautions to heart. I talked to other stunt people. Dar was a huge safety conscious stuntman. I learned the most from him.

While in New York, I worked on a few other films as well. Many of the stunt people I hired have gone onto bigger things. It was cool to think that I was a part of making their careers.

Back to Los Angeles. Things were still a bit slow. Still touched base with Stan. He was moving onto other things.

Our conversations were more about what he was looking forward to in the future. We talked about what he did for Marvel. I mentioned what Jack Kirby had said about creating Spider-Man. That one hurt him. He said that Jack was a huge part of co-creating many characters in the Marvel Universe, but Spider-Man was his brainchild. Even Jack's original sketches were far from what Stan had envisioned. He felt really bad about hearing Jack say Spider-Man was his creation.

I think Stan also tried to set me up with his daughter, Joanie. Stan asked me if I could set up his daughter's music system at her apartment. I agreed. Went there after talking to her on the phone. Joanie was stunning. My survival instincts kicked in. Do not go there. It could mess up a decent relationship with Stan. I put her stereo together, she made me a small pizza, I wolfed it down, and said my goodbyes. I might have been unintentionally rude to her. She was a bit distant with me after that. I had invited her to a play I produced and acted in at a nice equity tier theatre in Los Angeles. She was very short with me. Oh well, better safe than sorry.

In between gigs in Los Angeles, I got another call from Troma. "Toxic Avenger 2".

They needed me.

Now, I heard that Lloyd was not too happy with some of the other stunt coordinators he worked with since me. Some poorly executed stunts. One that went so bad the stuntman was almost killed.

They made me an offer I couldn't refuse. Financially, of course. So, I made my way back to the East Coast.

It was a bigger budget than any of the other Troma films. I had carte blanche on the stunts and the budget. Full on car chases and crashes. Motorcycle jumps, slides, and crashes. A fight at the end with both Toxie and the Devil on fire. It became so big they did a Salkind-type of deal where they split it into two movies.

Jumping, Burning, and Falling on the Toxic Avenger I II & III

We had a minor accident on the set that could have been catastrophic. I was lucky. The stuntman was lucky.

The scene was that the Devil drove a bus through a crowded picnic. He slammed into a car. The car either went into the picnic table on the left, or the one on the right. As soon as we saw what table the car was going to, we jumped out of the way and landed on the other table.

"Let's rehearse."

Walk-through.

"Hit." Car went to the left. The stunt man went to the right.

Again.

"Hit." Car went to the right. Stuntman went to the left.

We rehearsed it six times.

"Got it?"

"Got it."

"Action!"

Ok. For real with the actual bus and car as I drove the bus through the picnic grounds. Stunt people ran and dove out of the way as I came to the car.

Right as I was about to hit the car the stuntman bolted and ran for the table on the right.

I couldn't stop.

Wham.

Car was hit, and of course headed right for the table the stuntman ran to. Stuntman crashed on the table. Car rolled over what looked like him and the table. Bumped along before coming to a safe stop. The stuntman was on the ground. Looked dazed he moved in circles like Curly from the Three Stooges. (I thought, this is it. I am done in the business.) Another stuntman picked him up.

"No! Don't pick him up."

He dropped him.

"Don't drop him!"

He picked him up again. "No! Leave him alone!"

He dropped him again. The Three Stooges live.

The stuntman came out of his dazed stage. He looked at me and smiled. "Pretty good, huh?"

I said, "you are so lucky. You have no idea how lucky you were."

That was his last day on set. It could have been his last day in general.

I have since improved on many aspects of this type of stunt. One is using cables to send vehicles in a given direction. Admittedly, that would not have helped if the stuntman still went before impact and headed the wrong way.

Back to Los Angeles. I started hustling again. I met Jim Arnett, a top stunt coordinator and second unit director. He was working on "Police Academy VI". He hired me to double one of the main bad guys. I worked with the top echelon of the stunt industry. Many of whom later became friends.

I was also hired by Jim to work on "The Rocketeer". That was exciting as I knew the creator, Dave Stevens. We talked while he was on set.

My acting career became more of a memory. I was becoming a full-time stuntman. I was getting good at it. I started stunt coordinating on more projects. Got in with some very talented and capable people. Many are still friends today. Started doing more second unit directing.

I started meeting people I had only heard about. Folks like Gene Labelle, Jeannie Epper (Wonder Woman), and even Hal Needham, to name a few. These were legends in the industry.

I loved directing. It was an amazing creative outlet. I had learned from some of the best like Francis Ford Coppola, Steven Spielberg, Wes Craven, and Clint Eastwood to name a few.

Work was good, I was making good connections. Money was good as well. I started working on major motion pictures.

I had a few stumbles along the way. I was asked if I could pole vault.

I said, "I used to. Let me see what I can still do."

A stuntwoman I knew set me up with a track coach at USC that was fantastic. I picked it up again and got even better.

I called the stunt coordinator back and said, "Yes. I can do it."

I kept practicing as I had a few weeks before the shoot. All was good.

The movie was "Perfect Weapon". The day of the shoot, I arrived at the location. The height of the fence was what I practiced the vaults against, but it turned out they added barbed wire at the top that made it about a foot higher. I started to psyche myself out. My first run was a little off. I got up but did not make it over. The stunt coordinator was swearing and getting really angry.

This did not help.

Each run was worse than the previous. I even tore my hamstring a little. I thought, "It's over."

I called the stunt coordinator the next day and left a message about how sorry I was that I messed up. The stuntwoman who set me up with the coach and the coach as well were surprised to hear what happened. I was nailing it in practice.

This particular stunt kept coming back to haunt me for a few years. On a stunt audition for "Hook" (another story there), I ran into that same stunt coordinator. He was auditioning as well. He smirked at me and yelled back into the audition room, "hey you should hire this guy, He's a real good pole vaulter."

I would hear stories from time to time. The story would change and make what happened even worse.

A few years down the road I was talking to another stunt coordinator that was a friend. He brought it up as a joke. I forgot that they were close.

I said, "Do you want to hear his side, my side or the truth?"

"No, no. I don't need to hear anything."

I proceeded to tell him anyway. "I worked hard at this stunt. I had it down perfect in practice. On the day I thought I could do a great job, go home, and that would be it or I could mess up and he would remember me forever. What do you think?"

He laughed. Seeing the absurdity of it all.

Again a few more years later I was working on the Warner Brothers Lot . I ran into them both. My friend was standing next to the stunt coordinator I had messed up with.

"How did you get on the Lot?" my friend asked.

Looking right at the other stunt coordinator, I said, "I pole vaulted over the fence."

My friend laughed. As far as I know, that was the end of it. I messed up. I owned up to it. That's it.

Although, this stunt came back to me in a very serious and dangerous way.

There was a low budget movie, "Cyborg 2: Glass Shadows". It starred Angelina Jolie and Karen Shepperd. The stunt coordinator was a lady by the name of Kay Kimler.

There was a difficult, dangerous stunt where the stunt double for Sharon Shepherd had to jump from one building to the next. The jump was about 15 feet away to a lower roof. If she missed it, then it was a 70 foot drop to the ground. All the best qualified stunt women turned it down. Most of them recommended me. Not usual for a man to double for a woman anymore, but this was an extenuating circumstance. I met with Kay, sized up the stunt, said I could make it work. I wanted to stay away from using an air ram which is a device that launches the stunt performer through the air (I had not built mine at this time).

Another stunt man had done a similar stunt with a much smaller distance a few weeks earlier. Either he either mis-stepped or the ram mis-fired. Either way, he slammed into the adjacent building and fell 30 feet to the pads below. Seriously injured.

I worked out particulars. No way to use a wire pull. Nothing on either building could work as a rigging point. Running and jumping was a no-go. I needed something to propel me at a good distance and hit my landing every time, no matter what.

I was taking trampoline classes with a remarkable and talented man, Ray Zecca. He was a character. He lived trampolines. Amazing. I used to do some really cool tricks using a large sized trampoline. The double bounce would give me extraordinary height and distance. I talked to Ray about using a trampoline for this stunt. He thought it was great concept. So we mapped it out and started testing it. We went to an area and set up a long line of crash pads and tested my theory. And, sure enough, I was clearing the jump with four feet to spare on a good takeoff, two feet with a bad one.

This would work.

On the night, we took the trampoline in pieces up to the roof and set it up. Ray rechecked the area. He didn't like the lower level roof. We did not practice going to a lower level. There was another roof top on the adjoining roof with a small building on it that was very close to the same height. We pulled the trampoline over using ropes and set up the trampoline on the other roof. We were sure to measure out the distance. Pads in place. I did the jump. Perfect, on the money. Did it a few more times. Perfect every time. There was a neon sign that we could see behind me that said, "Jesus Saves". I fully believed it that night.

We pulled the trampoline back to the other roof. Set it. Waited for the stunt to happen.

We were ready for the shot. The first assistant director came up with Walkie in hand. He was the brother of the director.

Everything was ready. There was a group of stunt people below. One of them yelled up that there was an air bag deployed below. Don't worry. I yelled back, "if I miss, I will be bouncing off the building and fire escapes all the way down. Not sure how useful this will be, but thanks"."

We had an airbag set up on the other side. It belonged to my friend Paul Dallas and his partner Tom Davidson. They had their own stunt equipment company called Calculated Risks. Paul and I were close. He became one of the most important people in my life and career.

Our stunt coordinator, Kay, came up. She was visibly nervous.

I assured her, "I got this."

She went back down.

Ready to go.

The assistant director said, "when we roll cameras, when will you go?"

I said, "after I hear all three cameras are rolling, I will go on my own as soon as I feel set."

Perfect. "So, rolling, rolling, rolling, then you go?"

"Yes. Got it. Ready." I was bouncing, waiting for the camera.

"Rolling! Rolling! Rolling!"

I jumped a few controlled high jumps, I felt it, I had it. I jumped to the end of the trampoline, then the assistant director yelled, "wait!"

I buckled my knees to stop the forward momentum. He looked at me. "You have to wait for action."

At no time during our discussion did I hear anyone mention action. I was then a bit uncertain. I kept bouncing on the trampoline trying to get my rhythm back but I was off. I started again.

The assistant director said he knew me. Then realized I was the stuntman that messed up on "Perfect Weapon". His brother had directed, and he was the first on that one. He kept making remarks while I was jumping. Great, here we go again. What a waste. This guy was useless. He was definitely messing me up. At one point I completely blocked him out and felt it. I went. The jump was not perfect, but I cleared it with three feet to spare.

Kay came up. Said the camera was not fully focused. Asked if I could do it again. I was pissed. The assistant director made a dangerous situation even more dangerous. "So, no. not on your life. Or mine for that matter."

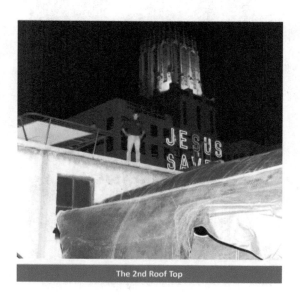

The 2nd Roof Top

The Practice Jump

The Actual Jump

Coming Down Towards the Air Bag

There was another incident later on that same movie that did not involve me where the stunt men were severely burned during an explosion stunt using air rams. I was lucky my stunt did not become an accident.

Back to "Hook". Everyone in town wanted to work on this Steven Spielberg feature. I mean everyone. I had years of practice with swords. I was very proficient. The stunt coordinator was a man named Gary Hymes. I have the utmost respect for this man.

Like everyone else, I had to audition. My sword skills impressed the sword master. The main choreographer asked me who I trained with. I said BH Barry, William Hobbs, and Victor Paul.

"Anyone good?" he asked. He could tell I was offended and he said he was just kidding. After my audition Gary said I was on board. Great.

I was also working on "Star Trek VI" at the time (a story there too).

A lot of stunt people asked me to work with them with swords. I obliged. I mentioned that Gary had all his people picked, but I guessed it couldn't hurt to have back up. One guy asked me what I thought of the sword choreographer on "Hook". I said, "we all have our own style. You just have to adapt".

"Star Trek" ended. I was waiting for my call for "Hook". Nothing. I kept hearing how hundreds of stunt people were being brought in. What the hell.

I went down to Columbia Studios and waited for Gary to come out. I wanted to know what happened.

About two hours later (I wasn't giving up), Gary came out. He went and talked to another crew member. As he walked by me, he stopped. "Hey Scott. Glad you came by, I want to talk to you. Hang out I'll be back."

This was encouraging.

A half hour later Gary came out. "My sword masters said you were bad mouthing him."

"That's not true."

"Look, we have both been in the business long enough that things can get twisted. I'll send him out to talk with you. If you can work it out, you'll be on the next rotation."

The sword master came out. He was a little defensive at first. "One of the stunt guys tells me that when he asked you what you thought of the sword choreographer you said we were not very good."

"Not true. What I said was, we all have our own style. You just have to adapt." Basically, the guy I trained told the fight guy a different version of what I said and got my spot.

"I know you were put off when I made a joke about who you trained with. No big deal. We are all entitled to an opinion." Somehow, we got on the subject of fight choreography and the history of swords. I had a book he was trying to find. It so happened I had two of them. I was glad to give him one.

We took care of our differences and like Gary promised, I was on the next rotation.

I will always remember how professional and friendly Gary was to me. He could have ignored me and moved on. He is a man of integrity.

Another stunt coordinator I have the utmost respect for is Vince Deadrick JR. He too comes from an iconic stunt family. His father, Vince Deadrick SR, was a well-respected stuntman.

I was hired to work on the Nickelodeon TV series "Victorious". I was brought out with my custom small air bag (more about this later). I also played an on-camera role as a stunt safety member. During the day of rehearsal, my wife was frantically trying to reach me. We had a rescue German Shepherd at that time. We all loved her dearly. I called back.

My wife said, "I think Shanti is dead."

"What do you mean?" I asked.

"She's laying outside by the front door. She's not moving."

"Try nudging her, sometimes she does that."

"I did. She's not moving. What should I do?"

"I guess throw a tarp over her until I get home."

She was upset. "I can't do that. I can't just leave her there."

Vince had overheard the conversation. He told me to go home. "Take care of this. This is only a rehearsal day. I got you covered."

I left to take care of my pup. I took her to our vet. They arranged a cremation for us. I went back to work.

Vince made a difficult time so much easier to deal with. This was not how our business usually worked. I will always hold a special spot in my heart for Vince. He knows this.

Forever In Our Hearts
Shanti
2002
2010

Back to working on "Hook".

That movie was one of the greatest experiences of my life. Huge fan of Steven Spielberg. I was going to see the man in action. The stage was tremendous. It had Captain Hook's ship, the lost boys, and pirates on the sound stage. After the big attack, I ended up laying on the stage as a dead pirate for about two weeks.

Gary was smart. It was a huge undertaking. He gave other stuntmen that he trusted groups to be in charge of. He handled everything meticulously and with style.

One day, Jim Arnett, who Gary had assigned as one of his helpers came to me and said, "Scott. You know rigging pretty well, right."

I did.

"I need you to go to Stage 25. I need you to do safety."

Damn. I wanted to see Spielberg in action.

I went to Stage 25. There was what looked like a large cuckoo clock and a very strange camera set up. Intriguing.

Julia Roberts came in and sat up on the clock. She was Tinker Bell. The camera was from Industrial Light and Magic. Their job was to enhance Tink's wings. They set up the shot, I had my hand on Julia's butt to steady her in place. There were safety mats, but our job was to keep her from falling. Another man handled the mats. I have said that my job description that day was as butt wrangler for Julia Roberts.

We hung out for a while. I had no idea what the hold-up was. Then, the door opened and in walked Steven Spielberg. He was there to direct Julia Roberts. I watched as he gave directions. Between takes he was on the phone with Harrison Ford. They even talked about stunts.

There was one time, Julia, Steven, Julia's assistant, and me were sitting on the floor between takes. We started talking movies. The new one was the Harrison Ford movie, "Regarding Henry". Julia's assistant thought it was fake. The time from when he was shot to healing was too fast. I disagreed. I said, "you could see time passing with the way the wound was healing. It showed the passage of time." Steven was impressed by my observation.

I felt like I got a private three-hour directing class with Steven Spielberg. It was incredible.

As I mentioned earlier, one of the strangest parts of working on "Hook" was for two weeks the entire pirate stunt team would lay on the stage being dead after the big battle scene with the lost boys. A few of the stunt people would be on their phones between takes. I would hear some of their whispered conversations. "No. I'm still here. Still dead. I have no idea how long we will be here."

Robin Williams would wade through the sea of stunt people laying there to get to the ship. Sometimes he would have funny remarks like, "guess you were dying to get into this business." Things like that.

I mentioned working with him many years ago on "The World According to Garp". He did not remember me.

I understand that Mr. Spielberg would change shots sometimes. I heard he had this idea that "I've seen where they swing a sword, and the lit candles blow out, but I never saw a shot where you swing a sword, and the candles get lit". Then there would be a delay as special effects would try to make it happen. Worked for us. Two weeks of work was a hefty paycheck.

Back to "Star Trek VI".

I met the stunt coordinator, Don Pike, at his office. He took a liking to me right away. He booked me as one of the crew members on

"The Excelsior". Captained by Sulu, played by George Takei.

We were beginning filming when I was playing a crew member. Our ship was supposed to be hit by an anomaly. We were thrown all over the place. (And in old Star Trek fashion, we shook, and threw ourselves around.) This was the start of the film.

Crew of The Excelsior

Basically, a three-day shoot. Dressed in Star Fleet uniforms, members of the original cast would come in from time to time. It was a Trekkies dream.

Between shots we hung out. was One time I was sitting next to Mr. Takei. We chatted a bit about the history of Trek. The diversity. I said, "Why was there never an openly gay crew member?"

"Well, uh. They were there, it just wasn't a big deal. Everyone fit in."

Then I started to joke, "Can you imagine?" I spoke in a very effeminate stereotypical gay voice.
"I'll take you where no man's gone before. I'll show you warp speed. Do you like what I did with the dylithium crystals? Don't they make a fabulous bracelet?" And so on.

George was in hysterics. He laughed in a big booming voice. Nicholas Myers looked over startled. "Oh, it's just George."

I did not know that George was gay. I was just having fun. I learned later from a close friend of mine, Richard Arnold, that not only was George gay, he thought I was hitting on him. I had run into George at a restaurant later on. We had a good laugh over it.

Richard was Gene Roddenberry's right hand. Like me with Spider-Man, he knew everything about Star Trek. He was an incredible encyclopedia of Trek information. He was a guiding force behind me working on just about all the various incarnations of the Trek shows. Unfortunately, cancer took him a few years ago. He was a good friend. I miss him.

Also, our stunt coordinator was having issues with some of the wire work. In another scene, the Klingon ship (called a Bird of Prey) was hit with a mechanism that shut off the gravity. So, Don (the stunt coordinator) decided to change out some of the stunt players that were having difficulties with the wires that made them look like they were floating. He asked us who was comfortable with wire work.

Three of us raised our hands. So he had us audition with the wires. A good friend of mine Don Ruffin went before me. Did a great job. Don Pike said perfect! Looked like he was going to move on. I said, "what about me? Let me try."

And Don Pike agreed. This is where my gymnastics came in handy. I would easily maneuver in the wires, and this landed me the part of The Klingon transporter officer. The other stunt people that did well on the wires got to play floating Klingons in the hallways, so we all worked.

The hours were long and exhausting. Wearing a harness under the heavy Klingon suit was difficult, made it impossible to take bathroom breaks. The scene was the ship getting hit. Gravity shut off, and we started to float. Assassins beamed aboard the ship. I was hit with a phaser and knocked back. Special effects came in and held these translucent pink balls in front of me to add Klingon blood later in post.

Then, I had to hang upside down for what seems like forever while Star fleet boarded the ship to see the destruction. I got a headache from that. Hanging upside down is no picnic. (I had done it in the past at a few Spider-Man events, but never that long.)

And then, just like with "Hook", I laid on the floor as a dead Klingon. Three days. I remembered a background performer made a snide remark about me getting an "easy job". Another friend of mine, Guy Vardam (He was doing background that day) who worked with Richard Arnold told him, "This guy has paid his dues. He has worked long and hard to get where he is." Now, that's what true friends are about.

I was pretty much working steadily. Things were good. Lot of TV, movies. Doubled some actors. Mario Lopez in "The Journey: Absolution". A few pictures for Ray Liotta. He could never remember me.

With Ray Liotta & Have We Met Before?

Dennis Hopper & Me

Worked with some legendary actors. Icons.

Frank Gorshin

Mickey Rooney

Billy Bob Thorton

Bridgette Fonda

And then there was Olivier Gruner in "Savage". He was a stickler for stunts. During a meeting with him prior to being hired, I showed him moves on the trampoline that I thought his character would do. He loved them. Afterwards he saw that my checkbook had an embroidered Spider-Man on it. "Oh, so that's where you got those moves?"

"In a way? Yes." Spidey was still in my blood.

We did a huge fight scene on a movie called, "Mercenary". Olivier was in it. So was John Ritter. I did second unit and actually got to direct John in one scene. John was a great guy. I was saddened by his sudden death.

John Ritter & Me on 2nd Unit

Between Shots on Set

I put together this kick ass fight sequence that the director, Avi Nesher, said was the best that Olivier ever did. The credits showed Olivier as the fight choreographer. Oh well. That's Hollywood.

I worked a lot for Avi Nesher. He is one of the most respected directors in Israel. At one point we did a movie called "Mars". Olivier was our star. He was giving a lot of attitude. Not happy to be there. Avi was the producer. Jon Hess directed. I love Jon. A true professional and someone I am proud to call friend. Avi came by the set. He had heard there were issues with our star. Avi was Israeli.

As I understood it all Israel citizens MUST do a tour of duty in the military. No exceptions. Avi was proud of his military service.

So, Avi took me aside. "I think I need to bring in an ex-military operative, big, muscular to maybe put our star in his place."

I said, "That might be good. Who?"

"ME," he exclaimed. "I am talking about me!" Avi is of a thin frame.

I did not picture him as the large, muscular, Israeli soldier he was talking about. But I said. "Oh, of course."

I also worked on "Lois and Clark the New Adventures of Superman". I originally doubled John Shea as Lex Luther after doubling him on a movie of the week. We got along well, and he requested me.

Doubling John Shea on A Movie of The Week

Later on, near the end of the series, I actually got to double Dean Cain. I wore the suit.

Me & Dean

My Very Pregnant Wife & Dean

Wally Crowder was the stunt coordinator. Wally was a pro with promotion. He knew how to put on a good presentation. Top of the line. He had a way with words. Wally was also the stunt coordinator on "Dexter" and "Desperate Housewives". Thanks to Wally, work was in abundance. Don't get me wrong. It was reciprocated. Some good jobs.

Wally and I would have our issues from time to time. However, in the end it was always forgive and forget. I can say that even though we are now in different parts of the country, we are still good friends. That is a rarity in this business.

Wally had also set me up with his good friend, Ellis Edwards. Ellis was the main stunt Coordinator for The World Wrestling Entertainment (WWE). I was able to work out some incredible stunts for them. Ellis would bring me in, usually for specific high work. There were times that the wrestlers jumped from heights up to 20 feet or more above the stage. It was my job to add a safety measure to the stunt to make sure it was safe for the performer. I would design special air bags that would be hidden under tables to help soften the impact. I also set up some fire burns for the shows. I am not at liberty to give full details on most of these as they are considered a trade secret by the WWE.

However, I can tell you about the first time that Ellis brought me in. The wrestler Shane McMahon was supposed to leap from the rafters to over twenty feet to the stage below and land on his opponent. Before he hit the stage, his opponent rolled out of the way, and Shane hit the stage. Ellis had come up with a concept of using a type of construction sheet that was lightweight thin wood. Boxes were underneath. The construction sheet was placed on the stage and blended right in to break Shane's fall when he hit it.

Sounded doable. Only thing…. Ellis wanted me to test it out first. OK… I got up to the top. Looked far. No pads or air bag below me. What looked like a solid floor. I was supposed to leap off and land on my back. This was like nothing I had done before. Blind faith jump onto what looked like a solid floor. Ellis told me not to worry. It would be soft and safe. I threw caution to the wind. I leapt. I hit the floor. HARD. It caved in slightly, but I never made contact with the boxes. It felt like my insides wanted to push out of every orifice. I was fine. Shaken up. Ellis discussed with Shane if he wanted to see it again. I thought with a smile on my face, "Dear God, please no".

Thankfully Shane said, "No, I got this."

Now, Shane was MUCH bigger and heavier than me. On contact the floor broke and he hit the boxes. So, yes, it was safe and soft, for a larger heavier person. Thankfully, that was the last "hard" stunt I ever did for them. We started using test stunt people who were closer to size and weight of the actual performers.

Me and Shane McMahon

CHAPTER
Eighteen

SPIDER-MAN RETURNS!
(AGAIN)

As I established myself as a stuntman in Hollywood, word came out that "Spider-Man: The Movie" would indeed get made. As I understood it, after Joe Zito left the project, they tried to get it up and running with Albert Pyun as the director.

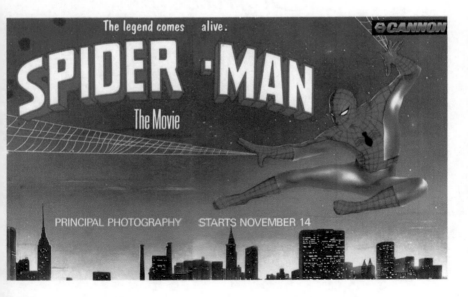

So, I figured what the hell. Here we go again. I sent my Spider-Man promo package to Albert's office. Nothing. Made calls. Nothing. Sent stuff to casting. Still nothing.

Then I got a call from my agent. "They are sending your headshot around asking for an actor that resembles you, only younger. They want to make Peter Parker fifteen."

"Too old for Peter, anything else?"

"Too young for Uncle Ben. Let's try stunts." At least I would still get a chance to work on it.

Called again.

"They have a stunt coordinator, Alan Gibbs." Alan was one of the most well-known and respected stunt coordinators in our industry. He was Jack Nicholson's stunt double for what seemed like forever.

Alan was a decent man. I had met him a few times in the past. I figured I'd give it a shot and reach out. So I called and left a few messages. Nothing. I was surprised.

At one point, I got a call from Spike Silver. Another good man. He said, "I'm taking over Alan's projects. Alan is very sick."

"I'm sorry. I did not know that." I had wondered why he hadn't returned any of my calls.

Spike was nice. "We're not too sure what is happening with Spider-Man, but stay in touch."

Alan passed away a few weeks later.

The project was cancelled following Cannon's acquisition by Pathé and Golan's departure from the studio.

Golan extended his option on Spider-Man as CEO of 21st Century

Film Corporation. By 1989, Golan attempted to revive the project using the original script, budget, and storyboards developed at Cannon. In order to receive production funds, Golan sold the television rights to Viacom, home video rights to Columbia Pictures, and theatrical rights to Carolco Pictures where James Cameron became attached to write and direct the film.

I sent a package to James Cameron at Lightstorm Entertainment.

A few months later I received it back.

I was uncertain why. So, I called. The person I was forwarded to explained they didn't accept unsolicited scripts.

I explained, "It's not a script."

"We know, it is a bunch of pictures and articles. (At least I knew they saw it). Mr. Cameron will not be doing this movie."

I went back to work as a stuntman (more on that later).

Meanwhile, after much back and forth for the next ten years the movie rights bounced around and finally Sony Pictures got them.

Once the picture was a go and they hired their director Sam Raimi, I started pushing again.

This time, I was pushing to be the stunt coordinator. I made calls. (Even to the head of Sony, Amy Pascal). Sam's office. I went to the studio in hopes of meeting with Mr. Raimi. Pretty brazen of me, but I was passionate about this character. Way too much history. I was not giving up.

Sam's right hand man was very helpful and extremely nice. I was also in communication with Kevin Feige a production executive on the film whom I met while working on X-Men. (More on that later as well).

Then one fateful day, I got a call from the producer Ian Bryce. Yes! Finally.

"We got your material, but I have already hired my own guy as stunt coordinator."

"I'm sorry to hear that. I have an extensive knowledge of this character I felt would be useful to this project. Specifically, the action."

"I know that. I agree. That is why I am having my stunt coordinator call you. I think he should work with you."
OK. Not bad. I'll go for that.

About ten minutes later, I get a call from the stunt coordinator, Jeff.

He was not too happy to talk to me, but as a courtesy to his producer, he did.

I congratulated him on getting the movie. He informed me he had been attached to the project for the past three months.

"Oh, I did not know that." I think he thought I was trying to pull the job away from him. Not the case.

"Well, I am extremely knowledgeable on Spider-Man. If, I can help..."

"I'm good," he said.

"Or if you can use an extra hand..."

"I am all crewed up."

End of call. To this day I do not think he cares much for me.

As production went on, Kevin Fiege and I would talk from time to time. We got to know each other pretty well, when we both worked on the first X-Men film. Me on stunts, him as assistant to Lauren Schuller Donner. I let him know what I was hearing. He would tell me some of what he knew. Nothing confidential of course.

At one point near the end of production, Kevin asked me, "Guess what The Studio is unhappy with?"

I said, "Tobey Maguire".

"No, what did you hear?"

"I heard (rumors only) that there was uncertainty about Tobey."

"No. The action. They don't care for the action."

"Specifically?"

"The fights. It's not the type of action that would befit Spider-Man. I am trying to see if they will bring you in. But it may be a long shot."

It did not happen.

The stunt coordinator brought in the stunt / fight choreographer he worked with on the TV series "Alias". John. One of the nicest people.

The end fight with the Goblin was reshot and The Studio was happy with it.

OK.

Back to work, back to my life.

Jumping ahead. Spider-Man was a huge success. They were gearing up for "Spider-Man II".

I figured I'd give it a shot again. I called the office. "Are you using the same stunt crew?"

"As a matter of fact, no. We are hiring Dan Bradley. Very excited about working with him."

I never worked with Dan before, but I had a good relationship with his two right hand men, Scott Rogers and Darren Prescott. I called Darren and said I would love to work with them. "I know Spider-Man. Probably better than anyone."

Darren said that they needed that and he would see what he could do.
Nothing happened. Never worked on any of the Raimi films. Wasn't meant to be.

I happened to run into Grant Curtis on the Sony Lot. Always nice and personable. I finally said, "I could never get in the door. What was the problem?"

He was very honest. "We liked you, but your credits were the main problem. You had mainly coordinated low budget films, and we would never be able to get those credits past Sony."

I appreciated that. It helped put a lot of things into perspective.

A side note on Spider-Man movies. After "Spider-Man III", Sony decided to reboot the franchise with Andrew Garfield in the lead.

I mentioned earlier getting a sense of approaching stunts in a more scientific way because of Dar Robinson. There were some drastic changes in both my life and the industry that made me look at changing safety equipment. At this point in time, I had started to develop some high-end state of the art stunt equipment. A friend of mine, Mark Dirkse (very talented rigger) called me to look at an air ram. They had purchased an old air ram from another stuntman that had purchased it from me when I had first started building them. I did my best to repair it but suggested they might use one of my newer models. They asked what I would charge. I said, give one day on the movie, just so I can finally say I worked on a Spider-

Man movie. The stunt coordinator, Andy Armstrong, said sure. We planned to use it in a few weeks.

A few weeks passed, and again, that did not happen.

Truthfully, Spider-Man was losing his appeal for me by then. Seemed like it would never be.

CHAPTER
Nineteen

LIFE OF A HOLLYWOOD STUNTMAN PART 3

I was working on more and more exciting projects. I was still coordinating low budget movies. I had a working relationship with an independent film company, PM Entertainment. Named after its founders, Rick Peppin (P) and Joseph Merhi (M).

I was called in to finish the stunt coordination for a movie that the stunt coordinator, Joe, had been working on. He did some high-end stunts but the problem was he was going way over budget, so they decided to replace him. It was a slippery slope. They convinced me that it was ok. The other stunt coordinator's stunt people were actually trying to get his job.

So, I agreed. The stunts went off great. Joe said he was going to use me on all his pictures from then on. When we finished the movie, they asked me what credit I wanted. I said, just put me down in stunts. The previous stunt coordinator had done most of the movie and some major stunts as well. The stunt coordinator credit was rightly his.

For Joe's next movie, he hired back his previous stunt coordinator. I never had a good relationship with that stunt guy afterwards. Sad. He did major features and was one of our top second unit directors.

Interestingly, my daughter and Joe's daughter went to the same school many years later. Joe and I reconnected. He always went on about how great his previous stunt coordinator was and how he had a part in helping him get there.

A year or two later, we were at the school graduation party. Joe and I were talking again. As usual he went on about his favorite stunt coordinator. He would be happy to hook us up.

I finally spoke up and told him that what he did back then hurt me career wise. "I replaced your guy at your insistence. You said I would work for you again. Not only did you bring him back, but by having me take his job over him made me look bad." I haven't had a decent relationship with his coordinator since. It's too bad. I really respected him. And, I am not sure Joe really understood this.

I'm glad I spoke up.

I met a lot of people working on these low budget films. One became my closest friend, and due to a tragedy, the inspiration for one of the biggest achievements in my life. Paul Dallas.

I was fortunate enough to work on some great shows. "Star Trek: The Next Generation", "Star Trek: Voyager", "Star Trek: Voyager" and "Star Trek Deep Space 9". I played a role with dialogue in "Soldiers of The Empire". I played Ortikan, a stunt acting role. The stunt coordinator Dennis "Danger" Madalone was probably one of the nicest, most warm hearted people I would ever know. A good thing too. I realized much later on that my manager had used a picture of a high fall that Dennis had done on my first composite. If I never said this, Dennis, you have my sincerest apologies and deepest respect.

A few stunt men had middle stunt names they were known by. Dennis "Danger" Madalone, Rick "Rocket" Neu, to name a couple. I was asked why I never used one. I joked that Scott "Butt Head" Leva would probably not get me very far.

Hey, if you can't laugh at yourself…

Dennis had called me in to read for a part on "Deep Space 9". When I walked into Paramount casting, all the other stunt men were 6'3" and above. They were massive, which is what a Klingon is expected to be.

I was 5'10". Well built, but definitely not Klingon built. I read for the part. I thanked them and left. On the way home my phone rang. It was Dennis. "You want to work on DS9 the next few weeks?"

"Really?"

"Yep. You got the part."

My acting background paid off.

It was a fun time. Long days. Incredible pay.

I wasn't a fan when I was a kid. As I mentioned earlier, I preferred "The Wild, Wild West". But I became a fan. Not a Trekkie, but a fan.

I actually got to work at least once on every Star Trek show when they rebooted them. Even got to work with the original cast on "Star Trek VI". I think that's cool.

I got stunt acting jobs from time to time. Television. A few soaps, "Lois & Clark", "Nash Bridges" and quite a few more, along with small movie roles.

All part of the job.

Things were going great. I was working steadily. Met a beautiful lady, Betsy, who would later become my wife.

Jobs were overlapping. I was interviewed for one film that some of the biggest stunt coordinators in town were up for. I was sure there was no way I was going to get it.

During the interview, the director talked about his ideas and concepts. I told him I thought they sounded great. My job was to make his vision with the action what he wanted.

I left. A few days later, I got a call. I got the job. I was the only stunt coordinator he interviewed that didn't tell the director what or how he should do things. The movie was called "The Independent". It was a parody that was loosely based on Roger Corman. The star was Jerry Stiller.

I thought it was a very creative concept. One stunt involved three stunt women crashing through a window. The director requested I use Julie Strain. No problem. I can make it safe. I sprayed, what is called "New Skin" on all the ladies exposed skin. Face, arms and legs to avoid getting cut when crashing through tempered glass. Julie's husband, Kevin Eastman came by to watch. We caught up on a few of our old meetings back at the Golden Apple and some conventions. He remembered me. The stunt worked great. Minor glass scratches. Julie did not like that, although it could have been worse with-out the skin spray.

Kept working. I hired people that hired me to pay them back. However, my main rule was, to first hire the right person for the job. Second hire the people that hired you, and third, hire your friends. My friends did not always work for me as the other spots would be filled. Some of my friends thought it should be friends first. I believe if I followed that train of thought my career would not have lasted.

I was fortunate enough to work with directors that really liked me and the way I worked. I tended to be the first on their list to be hired for all stunts.

One director, Mike, in particular summed it up for me. He was mainly a commercial director. I did many of *The Best Buy* TV spots. My first was, of all things, a Spider-Man video game spot with a very large actor. I designed a custom harness, so he could do the Spider-Man type action that was required. It worked great. Start of a beautiful working relationship with Mike and his wife who was the production manager. We even shot one at Paisley Studios near Minneapolis. Prince would peek out from the offices from time to time. They had a stringent rule, no meat inside the studios. If you had a sandwich with any meat during lunch, you would have to eat it outside.

Mike brought me in on another spot. It was for the AMC theatres "Silence is Golden" spot about turning off your cell phones in the theatre. It was based on a lake fight from the Jet Li movie, "Hero". By that time, I was using a lot of tools at my disposal. Books, behind the scenes videos, you name it.

There was a huge fight scene on a lake. The opponents hop across at each other and do a cool Kung Fu Crouching Tiger style fight. Special effects tell our director that the water fight is all CGI (computer generated imagery). I said, not so. It was all done practically.

Remember my tools?

Books in specific. I had a book on the making of the movie. It was in Chinese, but the pictures would show the action in detail. It was practical.

I told Mike I could do it. I used another tool of mine. One-sixth scaled figures dressed in traditional Chinese garb that looked like the characters. Using my pool, I mapped out the scene in photos. Mike loved it. We started getting ready to go.

Cut to our hero facing his foe across a lake from one another.

he prepares...

In a typical martial arts movie sort of way they run across the water and rise above it to battle.

They theatrically battle

Blocks, dodges, leaps etc.

His foe, twists the staff and our hero flies and flips.....

Landing on the other end of the staff.

We hear a ring........

What the.......

Our villain reacts...

Who splashes into the lake.

Spinning both his staff and our hero.....

As he falls the enemy looks down toward him.

The Best Buy logo rises, followed by the AMC logo

I sat in on the casting sessions. Simon Rhee, an incredible Martial Arts Master, was cast as the lead, and Paul Wu from Vancouver was cast as the villain. Jing Li from the US was cast as the wife. We left for Vancouver and got ready to shoot.

I hired an incredible rigging crew I had worked with in Vancouver in the past. We mapped out everything. Rehearsed, made adjustments. Started shooting. It looked spectacular.

I started working on the fight with Paul, while Simon was doing other shots. Simon stopped by and said, not to worry, he could do that later. He meant choreograph the fight. He was an incredible fight choreographer. One of the best. When he came back, I had already finished the fight. "You did that?" He asked. Yep. I was an experienced fight choreographer long before I did stunts. He was impressed.

One final shot dealt with Simon standing on Paul's fight staff on the lake. Phone rang and they were interrupted. Simon was thrown spinning into the lake. The director thought it best if we did this in cuts. I told him I could do the throw and spin hitting the lake in one shot. He let me work my magic. It went great. The whole shoot was like a big budget Kung Fu movie.

Another spot was shot afterwards. The local production manager had her local guy in mind. It was a James Bond type of sequence. Mike wanted me but decided to let the production manager use her guy.

The shoot was good.

After the shoot, we met for lunch in California. Mike told me how well everything went. Then he talked about the James Bond sequence. He said he and his director of photography talked about it. They liked it. All the stunts worked as scripted but something was missing. It was missing that extra Scott Magic that I added to the stunts. That made what we did special. He liked it, but unlike the lake sequence it was missing my extra creativity. That was one of the best compliments I could ever receive.

Thank you, Mike.

Time moved on and I was still working. Things were good. I was living with my future wife. I traveled a lot. She tended to go with me. Who wouldn't want to go to San Felipe Mexico or Ireland.

In 1994 we got married in Las Vegas. No Elvis wedding, but we did get a coupon for a discount at the Silver Bell chapel. Small wedding. Her dog Tasha was slowly going blind but regained her sight to be a witness at our wedding.

I was working nonstop. In 1997, I worked a film called "Spoiler" and then went to "Lois & Clark" that same day. I got a call from my wife. She was going to be induced. I had no idea how long we would be shooting. The scene was a gang in a shoot-out with police. Four of us were shooting out the second story window. All of it was shot on the Warner Brothers backlot. A red and blue blur zipped through behind us and we were thrown out the window. Special effects added the blur later. We ended up being the last shot of the night, around 2 AM.

My wife arrived at the hospital at 12:00. We did one take. Perfect. I hit the small airbag, heard them call it, "That's a wrap". I rolled out of the bag and rushed to the hospital in time to see my baby girl born.

Best day of my life.

One film specifically was being shot in Toronto. My wife and her family were there so this enabled her mother to spend quality time with her granddaughter. I had applied for dual citizenship which made it easier to work in Canada, so I was able to work there and be with the family as well.

I met the stunt coordinator, Gary, while working on a film in New York about a year before.
We got along. He was breaking down a script for a feature film called, "The X-Men" that was going to be directed by his guy, Bryan Singer. We talked shop. He liked my knowledge of the X-Men. I was not just a Spider-Man fan. I was pretty versatile with other Marvel heroes as well.

We met up again. He wanted me to work with him on X-Men. I had Canadian status and was a member of the Canadian union, ACTRA. When someone brought a US film to Canada, they needed to use what was known as a match. Another stunt coordinator who is Canadian had to be your mirror match basically. Gary wanted me to be his match.

This did not go over so well. It seemed as though the producers did not like or want Gary on the picture. Thankfully Bryan had his say in that matter. However, since they were not too fond of Gary, they were not too fond of the people he brought in. I was not hired as the match. They hired a local. I was put on a stunt utility contract and was given screen time as we shot.

It was a difficult shoot. One of the hardest and quite frankly miserable productions I have ever worked on. I almost felt like leaving the business afterwards. A lot of politics, back-stabbing, and just all-around unhappiness.

I was in charge of putting the Wolverine / Sabretooth statue of liberty head fight together. Interesting story. A stunt book was put out by a friend of mine who was a top stunt coordinator as well. Wally Crowder. It was called, "The Stunt Players Directory". It became the stunt bible as far as casting and finding stunt people and doubles. Very innovative.

I went through the book and showed prospective doubles for the main characters. Difficult, as none were really cast yet. Dugray Scott was slated to play Wolverine, and I was supposed to double him originally.

I showed various possibilities for a Sabretooth double, even though we did not have the actor yet. Surprisingly, the stuntman, Tyler Mane, was so perfect, he was cast in the role. Dugray was working on the latest Mission Impossible movie, and I do not recall what the issue was, but he would no longer be playing Wolverine. The hunt for another was on the way. In the mean-while I started working on the fight with Tyler. Kept it very comic book based. Tyler was a natural, and I was working as the Wolverine double.

Rehearsing The Statue of Liberty Fight with Tyler Mane

One of the producers, Tom Desanto, who was basically responsible for getting this movie made with Bryan Singer was a huge asset. Huge X-Men fan. X-Men to him, was like Spider-Man to me. Basically, X-Men might never had been made if not for Tom. Another friendship I truly value.

The filming started. The cast was in place. Except for Wolverine.

Then Marvel Promotions called. Been awhile. They needed a stuntman to go to Amsterdam to do an event for FOX that was opening a TV station or something there. I figured, what the hell. They needed a Goblin as well. I said, I would hire a stuntman if that was ok.

Checked to see that I could get away for a week. Ok. Still waiting on our Wolverine, so I had some time. Hired a friend who was competent in rigging. He would wear the Goblin costume as well.

Flew to Amsterdam the following week.

Amsterdam was a beautiful place. It is known for legal prostitution, live sex shows, and pot cafes.

I do not smoke pot and I am married. I might have been unfaithful in some of my previous relationships, but I looked at marriage as a whole other commitment.

I had a belief, "If you lie or cheat on your spouse, why would I trust you since you broke a solemn vow?" It might sound hypocritical, but I stand by that to this day.

I visited a pot café with my co-stuntman and our sponsor. I did not partake. She was nice. Suggested we take in a live sex show, just to see it. We did. Not really worth it. Not much of a story. Boy meets girl, boy eats girl... but I did see it just because we were in Amsterdam.

Walking along the river I saw prostitutes in the large windows, like products on display. No judgement. To each their own. It is well controlled by the government and seemed to work.

My big adventure before the event was a visit to Anne Frank's house. It was incredible. To see the house, to hear the story. It was the best part of the trip.

Now to the event. One of the heads of Fox from the States was there along with his Amsterdam head of Fox. For the stunt, I was supposed to crawl out of the third story window and crawl to the street where I would do a meet and greet with everyone involved.

My guy rigged it. As I said, he was competent, but if I had to do it again, I would have brought a more seasoned rigger. I had to keep yelling instructions to him as I crawled down the side. Too much slack, slower, faster. The crowd below would repeat what I was saying. Kind of embarrassing.

It looked cool. I looked like Spider-Man crawling down the side of the building. When I got to the street, I flipped my legs over my head, unclipped from the harness, and met the crowd. Then I went inside.

Once inside our sponsors wanted us to do a confrontation between Spidey and The Green Goblin. Ok. Two stunt guys could go at it pretty good. But wait. No violent body contact, no hits to the head. Keep it clean. That was not allowed in Amsterdam (Excuse the language here). So, I said to our sponsor, "I can get the Goblin stoned and fuck him, but no physical violence?"

She laughed and said, "Exactly".

Ok. I flipped around, did spin kicks, wide punches, all of which the Goblin ducked and avoided.

Then I grabbed his arm and flipped him to the ground. He got up and ran away. All in a days work. Easy money.

It was an interesting event.

Back to Toronto. Back to X-Men.

Once I returned, I saw they found their Wolverine. A 6'3" Hugh Jackman that was one of the nicest actors I have ever worked with. He would often say I helped him become Wolverine. Truth is, I helped, but he brought life to Wolverine. How else could a 6'3" man take a 5'6" character and believably make him his own? I have so much respect for Hugh. He is always so kind and welcoming. One of my best times on the film was working with him.

I worked with him on the choreography. He was great. I would no longer be able to double him due to our extreme size difference. So, I found a decent enough double out of Vancouver. A bit full of himself. The double took to the choreography well but was not too keen on the wire work I designed for the fight.

The fight was right out of a comic book. I had slashing, stabbing, throwing around. At one point they were both lying next to each other mid fight. Sabretooth grabbed Wolverine and slammed him three times back and forth before throwing him off the head. Wolvie caught one of the statues, spiked on the crown, and swung back onto his head.

I designed this to be practical. The stunt men needed upper body strength and some gymnastic skills. The rag doll throw would be done with a one-handed handspring with an assist from the rigging team. Same with the swing around on the crown which required a one-armed giant swing with a wire assist. Not so easy. But I knew that since I could do it, it was possible.

Rigging wasn't sure where the wires would go. When we put together a car chase sequence for the film, we brought our toy cars and with everyone involved showed where the action would happen. This helped set up cameras and gave everyone an idea how this would work. Pretty standard prep-work.

Now, we couldn't use a toy car to show this type of action. So the question became, "What to do, what to do?"

I went to the local comic shop and bought a six-inch Wolverine action figure and a twelve-inch Sabretooth.

Then, like I did during my childhood, I played out the action. Showed them where the pick points on the harness would be, where the overhead rig would sit, and where they would pull from. This came in handy in the future and it worked great. During set up before the new Wolverine double joined our crew, we executed a perfect fight.

Then a problem arose. The producers heard there were issues with the statue fight. None that I knew of.

We were asked to demonstrate the fight in front of the producers and director. I heard that they were questioning who I was, and why I was doing the fight.

I had Hugh work with the Sabretooth double. I did the fight with Tyler first. We showed what it was supposed to look like, then Hugh, who was still working on it, stepped in and did his. Pretty good.

Then Bryan hemmed and hawed. He wasn't too sure. Thought it needed to be more violent (Guess he hadn't been to Amsterdam). Producers decided to bring in a Hong Kong stunt team for the Wolverine / Mystique fight, and a 2nd Unit Director to take over the statue fight. Cory Yuen came in with his fight team. Among his team was Ke Huy Quan. Short Round from "Indiana Jones and the Temple of Doom", "Goonies", and the recent best supporting actor Oscar winner for "Everything Everywhere All at Once".

They started working on the Wolverine/ Mystique fight.

Another top Stunt Coordinator / 2nd Unit Director, Conrad came in as 2nd Unit Director and started to change the fight. More body slams, more hits.

I was asked to come in with the statue wire stunts. The stunt double could not get it. Conrad was getting pissed. They just couldn't do it. So he asked, what was the problem. Gary was there. He did not like Conrad. I asked Gary to let me put on the harness and show them. He said no.

I went back to my unit with Cory Yuen.

At one point, I walked passed Conrad's Office. I got along with Conrad. I liked him. He brought me in and showed me a few things. Mentioned he was bringing in a double for Mystique. Vicki. Showed me a letter from Fox. Said that the statue head fight looked more like WWE wrestling. Were they talking about my fight or the new one? I shrugged like I don't know. The new one. It lost all its comic feel. They no longer did the ragdoll smash, and the crown swing was animated.

Too bad.

The Mystique fight was very Hong Kong. Some of what I saw I had seen in some previous Corey Yuen movies.

I had the concept of using a contortionist. She kept morphing into things, the wall, boxes whatever was nearby. At one point Wolverine swiped at her, she ducked, went between her legs, grabbed Wolverine's ankles and flipped him into a wall. Then she bounced all over the place changing, clipping Wolverine all the while. At one point, Wolverine closed his eyes, sniffed her out, and slashed her. Very comic style.

Cory had Wolverine run from the fight. Why? He was trying to rescue Rogue. OK. Not what would happen, but I had no say in the matter.

I talked to Tom Desanto. I said, "Wolverine would finish business, then move on".

Tom agreed. He spoke with them. There were some minor changes.

This was where I met and became friends with Laura Schuler Donner's assistant. I mentioned him earlier, Kevin Feige. He was a full-on comic aficionado and knew Marvel better than anyone. We would have cool in-depth conversations at the time.

Kevin is now the President of Marvel Studios. He singlehandedly turned superhero movies around and brought Marvel to the top. He stayed with basics. Impressive.

I can't get the time of day from him anymore, but I don't take it personally. He is busy. He has a studio to run. I'm not saying I wouldn't be excited to work on a Marvel show. I get it. I have much respect for him as well.

X-Men was getting to be more of a chore, than a fun-filled movie. It was exhausting. Conrad was getting complaints from the studio about everything he did. Bryan was complaining to them.

So, Laura Schuller Donner brought in the big guns. Richard Donner, her husband. Bryan became more subdued. During the shoot, they asked Richard what he thought. "Looks good to me," he said. Ok. Moving on.

There was a time I got to sit with Richard. We talked about Superman. He actually remembered me. We talked about Alex Stevens. It felt good.

He left after about a week.

I decided to have some fun. With Tom Desanto's help, we arranged for a special appearance while the X-Men entered the Statue of Liberty Museum. While Storm, Cyclops, and Jean ran in close to camera, a red and blue figure ran in behind them.

Dressed as Spider-Man, I officially made the first movie appearance as our webbed friend. "I am so sorry, I am in the wrong movie," I said as Spidey, then I turned and ran out.

Cyclops (James Marsden) ran after me.

Everyone laughed. It was a welcomed relief. The clips can be seen on YouTube or the DVD easter egg on the first release.

After X-Men, I returned home.

Spider-Man Visits the X-Men Set

Work was still booming. I did a movie in Jamaica. Lot of fun. The family was with me, of course. This was a "Tales from the Crypt" movie. I worked with a company I had done a lot of movies with. Avi Nesher was the main producer and director. He and his wife, Iris, had a daughter close to my daughter's age. They are still friends to this day.

I worked on a film adaption of the hit play, "The Fantasticks". My dad had told me that he went to college with the creators, Tom Jones and Harvey Schmidt. My dad played drums for Tom Jones student council campaign. I was to double El Gallo and jump from a high tower into a small bucket of water. I introduced myself to them. They were so excited. They remembered my father and were so happy we came full circle from my father, to me. It was fun.

On the Set of "The Fantasticks" with My Dad's Old College Buddies

One of my closest friends, my best friend, was Paul Dallas. Paul worked with me on almost every one of my projects. He was with me on the rooftop jump for "Cyborg 2". On one movie, "Deadly Target,", I had what was supposed to be a 100 foot high fall. I used Paul's 100' rated bag which was a large bag that was 20' x 25' x 10'. Paul came out with me to the location a week before the stunt. He measured the height. Yep, 100 feet he said.

I practice out at the park where there was a light tower that was just under 80 feet. No matter how many times I had done a stunt before, I still practiced. It was smart. It kept me safe. It kept me alive.

The stunt coordinator was a very good fight choreographer. I had worked with him in the past on some Cynthia Rothrock movies and "The Power Rangers" TV series. I played a Putty and doubled the Red Ranger.

Power Rangers

The window on the 9th floor I was going to crash through was a few feet back from the ledge. It made visibility difficult. I could not fully see the air bag until I crashed through the window and cleared the windowsill. I had Paul with me as my "point" man.

"What do you think?" I asked him.

"I would do it," he answered.

"I KNOW you would. I'm asking about me," I replied.

While production was elsewhere, I decided to try some practice jumps. A group of stuntmen who were close friends of mine came out to support me and even stand safety around the bag. Our director, Rick Peppin, came by. He wanted to set cameras to see what the best angles were for the fall. So I went up and I did a few more. 50', 75'. Then one just under the window I was going to jump through at 90'.

All was set, then an interesting thing happened. Jeff Imada came by the set. He is Japanese / American and a very well respected stunt coordinator. I heard a bunch of whispering. I asked our stunt coordinator what was going on. He said, "Nothing really. Jeff is here to scope things out. The man you're doubling is Asian"."

I said, "What!!!?" I had no idea.

I went outside, found Jeff. We had known each other for a while.

I apologized and said this was the first I heard this. He said it wasn't a big problem due to the height and particular specialty of the stunt, but he just wanted to check things out to be sure. I appreciated that.

Returning to the stunt, the time came to make it happen. I went to the top floor. I was told after cameras rolled and action was called to go on my own cue.

Here we go.

Cameras rolled... action.

I crashed through the window. I saw nothing below me but black. The bag was pure black, the lights set up around the bag for the shot were blinding. I felt a small acceleration in my descent. I rotated.

Oops.

Too early. I was a good 40 feet above the bag, and I started to over rotate. I came in at an angle instead of fully flat on my back. My instincts took over. Right as I hit the air bag I balled up tight so as not to injure my back. No problem. Safe landing.

Paul later told me the fall was actually 150 feet. There was a large 25 foot doorway with an arch at the front. He didn't want me to be nervous and knew I could do it. I would have preferred to know. Always check and double check your stunt yourself before you do it.

Paul died a few years later while performing a high fall on a TV series. It was devastating to me. It changed my life and even the industry.

CHAPTER
Twenty

GONE, BUT NOT FORGOTTEN

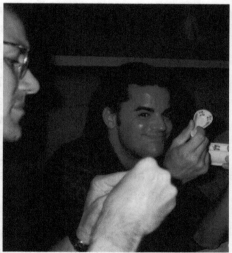

Paul Dallas

As I mentioned earlier, Paul worked with me a lot. I brought him on to most every project I did. When I directed pick-ups for a film early on, he was my stunt coordinator.

Paul was at a surprise birthday party my wife threw for me. He opened up about his family and some of his relationships. My wife is Canadian. Her sister was at the party as well. Paul spoke about an old girlfriend he was crazy about. Canadian. He married her to help her get her green card. The relationship did not work out. Sadly, they split. My wife's sister said, "But she got her green card still, right?" I thought, "THAT'S what you got from his story?"

Paul was very down to earth. He loved stunts, but he loved life equally as much.

While I was doing films for Mahogany Pictures, he worked with me. He actually played a role in one of them, "Gangster World".

The last picture we worked on was a feature called, "Mars", which was another Olivier Gruner film.

I had set up for a big fire stunt that night. I was playing one of the goons in a bar fight. A funny moment happened prior to the fire stunt. There was a card game in which my stunt people were all sitting around the table and the action called for Olivier to stab one of the players in the hand with a knife. I hired a stuntman from a group called, "Stunts Ability". They all had some form of disability. Dave Smith was our stuntman. He was missing his right hand. I worked it out so Olivier would stab his right hand, a prosthetic. Olivier was adamant that his character would stab him in his left. This became an ordeal. The left was real, right was fake. Finally got Olivier to agree.

He stabbed Dave's prosthetic hand, fight broke out. Knives, guns, and a flame thrower. I was supposed to jump at Olivier from the bar as the flame thrower fired at him. He dodged, I got fully engulfed in fire. Full burn.

I set up the burn stunt pretty easily. Had safety people in various areas, all with fire extinguishers. I was going to land on a table with kerosene on it. The table would ignite. Table was supposed to topple. If the table moved forward on impact, the man in front would be the first to extinguish me, if it moved to the left then guy on left, and so on. Rehearsed it. Everyone moved right on cue. Table to the left! Left came forward. Right! Right came forward. I had six people on extinguishers. No matter what, all were supposed to merge on me and hit me with extinguishers.

It was going to be a hot burn. I wore protective undergarments that had been soaked in fire gel. I had fire gel on my face, no mask. It would last about five seconds on the hot table before the flame from the table would dry it up.

When I was lit, I counted to three. On three, I moved in. "Okay, when you hit the mini trampoline," said the director.

"Noooo. When I am lit. It is a three second burn. Once I hit the table we are done."

OK. Everyone had it.

Ready. Roll cameras, action. I was lit, I hit the trampoline, one... I hit the table, two... the table ignited and slid across the floor, three... I was on the table, flames licked my face, I struggled to get the table to turn over. 4... 5... 6... 7... 8... 9... "PUT ME THE FUCK OUT!"

The table turned over, my stunt team all came in and hit me with extinguishers. It seemed they were all mesmerized by the stunt. My face was hot. I felt the burn, I had first and second degree burns, and was rushed to a nearby hospital. Treated. Came back. I was ok. My face would scab up a bit. Nothing too serious.

Paul was there. I asked him if he would like to work the next day, Friday, August 2, 1996.

He said he couldn't, he was bringing an air bag out for "Uncle Cole." Cole was the name of the stuntman Paul worked with a lot as well. I suggested he have someone else deliver the bag and hang with me. I wished he would have listened to me.

The next day while shooting, I got a phone call from one of our stunt answering services. (Before cell phones we had services, and a beeper to notify us for work.) I got to the phone. The girl from the service was in tears. She mumbled, "PawDullsmssdthbg".

"What?"

"Paul Dallas missed the bag. It's serious he's at the hospital. It doesn't look good. We are trying to reach his parents. No one knows how to find them."

I did not realize I was on my knees. My legs had folded.

I got another message. My wife had been trying to call. I talked to her. She has been on the phone with the hospital. "It's bad." She told them she was a family member, so she was able to get more information.

It was serious. Paul had done the fall (he wasn't supposed to), hit the edge of the bag, and gone to the ground. The back of his head hit a rail. His skull had separated from his spine. He was on life support until they could reach his parents. I was able to get the answering service to get in touch with his old stunt partner, Tom Davidson.

The rest of the night was like I was in a dream. I finished setting up the final shot on the film, gave another stuntman on my team directions on how to finish, and with another stuntman who was also a close friend of Paul's, Ed Anders, headed out to the hospital. We arrived a little after 5:00 am. Paul had passed half an hour earlier. His parents had been notified.

My world changed.

One of Paul's Obituaries:

SANTA CLARITA

A memorial service for stuntman Paul Dallas, who died after

suffering massive head injuries while performing a stunt last week, will be held Saturday.

Dallas died early Saturday at Providence Holy Cross Medical Center in Mission Hills after he fell three stories from a platform—missing the air bag that was to break his fall—while filming a stunt for the television series "L.A. Heat". He was 34.

Born Sept. 1, 1961, in Levittown, Pa., Dallas was always interested in the entertainment industry, his family said. During high school, he began to focus on stunt work and acting, and he later studied directing and producing at UCLA.

In 1982, Dallas visited Los Angeles, where he had his first lessons in stunt work. By 1984, he had moved to Los Angeles to begin his career.

After a period of struggle, Dallas' career began to flourish. During his career, he racked up more than 50 feature film credits, including "Stargate," "Major Payne," "Sister Act 2" and "The Beverly Hillbillies."

Dallas' television credits include "Melrose Place," "Dark Justice" and "Walker, Texas Rangers." He stunt doubled for actors Timothy Hutton, Jan-Michael Vincent, Eric Roberts and Matthew LeBlanc, among others.

In addition to his work as a stuntman, Dallas was a successful businessman. In 1986, he founded Calculated Risks, a safety equipment company that specialized in developing, designing and renting—ironically—air bags and other stunt-related equipment.

Dallas is survived by his parents, Joe and Anne Dallas of Levittown; a sister, Patricia Dallas Sharkey of Wilton, Conn.; two brothers, Joseph Dallas Jr. of Levittown and Michael Dallas of Wildwood, N.J.; and two nieces.

Burial will be in Levittown.

About a year earlier we lost a stunt woman, Sonia Davis, to a high fall stunt on the film "Vampire in Brooklyn". She had hit the end of the bag and bounced off, hitting her head on the wall behind her.

Premier magazine did an article about this. Paul was interviewed as a high fall / air bag expert.

Paul's death was the motivating factor for me to reevaluate the way stunt air bags worked.

After his funeral, and meeting his family, I helped his father sort various things out. They decided to liquidate Paul's equipment. Quite a few stunt people were interested. With the help of another stuntman, we were able to work out a deal to obtain all of Pauls' stunt equipment. We were asked not to use the name of his company, *Calculated Risks*.

We came up with a new name, *Precision Stunt Safety Specialists*. And we were in business.

Precision Stunt Safety Specialists Was Open for Businesst

I started playing with air bag designs. Looked at standard bags, looked at what Paul did. My partner preferred I let it go, and we keep things the way they were.

I had purpose, a reason. Why, if a person hits an air bag off center can it bounce or slide the performer out of the bag? There had to be an answer. I needed to find it. And I did.

With extensive research, and thousands of dollars in cost, my first new air bag was ready to go. Almost a year to the date of Paul's death, I had made a new, better, and safer air bag.

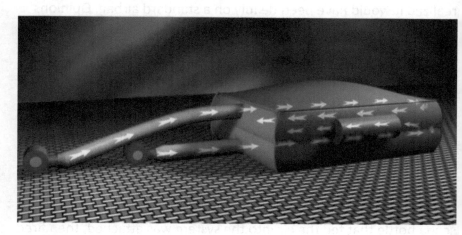

The standard air bag has a forward air flow with a sideways baffling system that caused the bag to bubble up. This could become a hazard as the bag could slide or bounce the faller out. Most air bag injuries or deaths had occurred due to this.

My design had an upwards flow system that kept the bag tight and flat and the faller in the bag. In fact, if the faller hit off center, the bag rolled the performer in towards the bag, not outside.

Doors started to open. I introduced the air bag to the stunt community. At first, I got a no big deal attitude. Pretty soon afterwards a few stunt people had a close call using my air bag. They realized it would have been deadly on a standard airbag. Opinions started to change.

Then I worked on other types of improvements to stunt equipment. I had mentioned air rams earlier. They were often called "Leg Breakers". The force of air that was used to propel the performer was massive. It would take between 2,000 to 2,500 PSI to throw a performer 10 to 15 feet. If the performer hit it wrong, it buckled his knees. It hurt.

I came up with a lighter, softer throw style of air ram that used very low pressure. Sometimes below 100 PSI. With a regular air ram, a scuba bottle that fed the air into the system was attached, then fired when stepping and triggered the ram. Or this was done leveraging a handheld button. In most cases, the performer would get five, maybe six throws before the bottle was switched out.

With mine, using very minimal air, we got between 100 to 125 throws before switching the bottle. This was unheard of. And it was sleek.

With the help of a very good friend who was also a top stunt coordinator, John Moio, I was able to get a testing ground for my new inventions.

We used it on a lot of shows. "Buffy the Vampire Slayer" used it quite a few times. Of course, the movie, "Flags of Our Fathers" used it too.

It has been John Moio's go-to stunt apparatus. He had always been my biggest fan. He bragged it was the best in the business.

Bob Yerkes, another famous stuntman, had a home that was called Yerkes Circus. He let us set up there on weekends. Test air bags, test air rams, you name it.

Bob has a big heart. He was welcoming and helpful. Many a stunt person or even just someone in need could find a place to stay at Bob's. There was an old joke, "What do you call a musician without a girlfriend? Homeless." I changed that to, "What do you call a stunt person without a relationship? Bob's guest."

Bob's place, with the guidance of John Moio, became a testing ground, and even a training facility. A lot of top stunt people came from there due to John's training and guidance.

Me & John Moio

All this ingenuity because of Paul.

Live shows started calling. Universal Studios, Disneyland, and Cirque Du Soleil.

I spent more than a year working with Cirque Du Soleil. They had a concept where they wanted a massive air bag to sit on a net and catch multiple falling performers. One right after the other. Could I do it?

"Yes, I can."

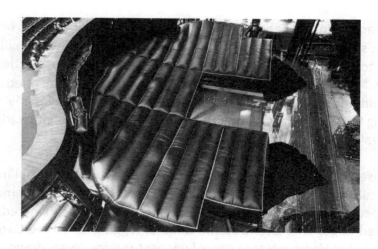

I designed a special air bag which was a series of airbags that had the blow out ports pushing air into the adjoining bag. It caused a ripple effect which made each bag adjust per faller. It worked and is still in use today.

I was also asked to let them try my new air ram for possible use in the show. It was fully tested by some of the Montreal stunt men. Most of whom I worked with on a Dolph Lungren film, "Minion", a few years back. It was an experience. I had to fight for my job. Constant backstabbing on that one, so I was a little nervous about their feedback to say the least. They were extremely positive, and very impressed. One of the Cirque show creators used the term, "sexy". Not bad for an improved version.

The lead rigging designer, Jaque Paquan, was difficult to read. I wasn't sure if he liked me or hated me. After the show was finally ready to open, we went to a celebration party. Jaque was a little drunk. "I came up with this concept. Afterwards? I was terrified it would not work. I thought I would fail big time. You saved my fucking life." That was as good as it gets. My design and innovations were taking off.

Because of this relationship with Jaque and Cirque in general I met a lot of talented people who designed and created some of the most spectacular sequences I have ever seen. Tony Galuppi, an incredibly talented rigger who later became Head of Rigging for all the Cirque shows in Las Vegas became one of my best friends. Years down the road, I brought him in on movies and commercials that I stunt coordinated. He had the most incredible mathematical mind where he could figure out how best to execute a special flying stunt or anything with rigging in general.

He had me work as a rigger on a local Cirque show In Los Angeles. I took the job part time as most of my afternoons were dealing with submissions for film and TV work. The "Day Player" position made it easier for me to leave for industry jobs whenever I needed. I also learned more about rigging than I ever knew before. I had to be certified with almost any new skill learned. It was eye opening. I learned so much about rigging and safety. It was an incredible experience.

I also got contracts with Universal Water World and Disneyland (Fantasmic). It was a dream come true. Paul would have been proud.

And the inventions were a boon to our industry. Since its inception, my airbag has saved the life of over 38 performers. My air rams have been instrumental in helping with difficult stunts where wire rigging was impossible to use. I am very proud of these accomplishments.

But, it gets better.

CHAPTER
Twenty One

AND THE OSCAR GOES TO...

Since the first day I introduced the new innovative air bag, I was told I should submit it the Academy of Motion Picture Arts and Science, Scientific and Technical Achievement Awards. I was busy. Between work and family, taking the time to fill out paperwork and submit it was not on my list of things to do.

Work was great. It was non-stop for a while. We bought our first house in West Hollywood, a condo. We purchased from John Calley who ran Sony Pictures at one time, and his wife, Meg Tilly. One of our neighbors was Curtis Hanson, Academy Award nominee for "L.A. Confidential". Another neighbor across the street was my friend from "Star Trek", Richard Arnold. Later we moved up to a house in the Hollywood Hills, and finally Studio City.

Couldn't be happier. My wife and daughter visited Toronto a few weeks out of the year to see family.
Interesting story. When Betsy and I first got married, she did not want to tell her family. She wasn't really ready for marriage and did not want to share this with any of her friends and family. I should

mention that she is Chinese-Canadian. Her mother and father had immigrated from China. Her father had passed away before we were married. (Our daughter, Georgia, is named after him, George).

So outside of telling my family, we did not tell her's. I visited sometimes but I was kept away from her mother. One visit, I was finally introduced to her. Not sure what changed. Her mother treated me very nicely. She only spoke Chinese. She kept pushing food at me during dinner. Told Betsy to fill my tea, get me more rice. Things Betsy was not too happy with. (She is not the stereotypical Asian submissive wife serving her husband).

Before we left, Betsy told her mother (with her sister Liz translating) that we were THINKING of getting married. Her mother said that was good. "Don't do a big wedding. Betsy's other sister had a big wedding, and it failed. Her brother too. Failed as well."

After a short pause, Betsy told her we were already married. Small wedding in Vegas.

Her mother replied.

"What did she say?" I asked Liz.

She said, "OK. Have a good flight. Welcome to the family."

Later, my daughter was born. My mother was ecstatic. She had a baby girl in the family. All boys before that. My brother had boys. My father was all boys in his generation and his father as well.

A little story about that. My wife wanted to know the sex of the baby early on. We set up an appointment for an ultrasound a few months down the road. My mother was excited about this. On the day of the ultrasound, my mother called.

"Well?" she asked.

"Well," I answered.

"How is Betsy?"

"She's good."

"And the baby?"

"Good, too."

"You were going to find out if it was a boy or girl today," she said.

"Yes." (Pause) "It's a boy."

My mother was disappointed. "Oh. Yeah. I thought that might be the case." (I am so mean.)

"Mom. It's a girl." She literally screamed with delight. I swear I could hear her dancing a jig on the other end of the phone.

Betsy's mother was very happy. That said, it was important to have a boy in the family. Betsy had two sisters, but finally got a brother. I don't think Betsy's parents were giving up until they got a boy. But her mother could care less with our little girl. She finally had a grandchild she could show off. It was a win, win for me.

So, every other year we visited for the holiday. We were sure to split the holidays between visiting the grandparents.

Later, Betsy and Georgia visited the grandparents yearly. I stayed home and worked.

In 2005, I had some free time. I was preparing for a feature that was a long way away. I looked at the submission form for the Sci Tech Awards at the Academy. It asked a lot of questions. I answered and put a very detailed submission together.

First week of September, I received a letter from the Academy saying my submission had been approved for consideration. They would send me further instructions on how to set up a demonstration.

The first week of October I received my second letter with instructions for the demonstration.

September 28, 2005

Mr. Scott Leva
Precision Stunt Safety Specialists
P.O. Box 40022
Studio City, CA 91614

RE: PRECISION STUNT AIR BAG

Dear Mr. Leva:

As promised, here is some further information for you concerning the Scientific and Technical Awards Demonstrations that will be held on Tuesday, October 18, 2005.

The demonstrations will begin at 7:30 p.m. on the stage area of the Linwood Dunn Theater located in the Academy's Pickford Center. The Pickford Center is located at 1313 N. Vine Street in Hollywood, California. The theater will be open at 2:00 p.m. and you can set-up your equipment at any time between then and 5:00 p.m. during the day. You must complete set-up by 5:00 p.m. You may park in the lot directly behind the Center (enter off of Homewood Avenue.) Check-in with the guard at the door where your name will be on a list. After receiving your credentials, proceed to the theater in the front of the building--I'll meet you there and show you where to set your equipment. If you have any special needs (i.e. power requirements, film or slides, heavy or bulky equipment, etc.) please let me know as soon as possible and we'll try to solve any problems before they arise. I also need to know right away who will actually be speaking during your presentation and their title, if applicable.

As you will see on the enclosed schedule, your 15-minute (maximum) demonstration has been slotted from 7:30 p.m. to 7:45 p.m. The hour preceding the demonstrations (6:30 – 7:30 p.m.) is a hands-on period and many of our committee members will arrive early and have questions regarding your entry. You should plan to be around your equipment or materials no later than 6:30 p.m. After the demonstrations begin there can be no further discussion. The demonstrations should end about 9:45 p.m. and you can take your equipment or materials out of the theater at that time. Equipment may not be left in the theater overnight.

(Continued)

On October 18, I went to the parking lot at the Academy's Pickford Center to set up my demonstration with John Moio and a couple of very capable stuntmen to help me demonstrate.

Early on, almost immediately after I received the letter of consideration from the Academy, I received a call from Discovery Canada. They were producing a documentary about the Sci Tech awards and wanted to include me. Of course. Who would turn down free publicity?

Air Bag Demonstration for The Academy

The demonstration went perfectly. I had my jumpers hit the bag off center. Jump two at a time, even three. I demonstrated that my bag did what no other air bag did before it. Good response.

One of the committee members asked, "Why not just use a bigger bag?"

I made a joke and said, "Contrary to what you heard in the past, but in this particular case, size really doesn't matter. Even if they hit a larger bag off center, it will bounce, slide or spit you out. These bags, which I have in all sizes, keep the jumper in, no matter where they hit, so long as their main body mass is within the bag. Even on the far corners."

Received good feedback. Now like everything I had done in the past, all I could was wait.

Right before Christmas of 2005, I received another letter...

Officers

December 21, 2005

Mr. Scott Leva
Precision Stunt Safety Specialists
P.O. Box 40022
Studio City, CA 91614

Re: Technical Achievement Award

Dear Mr. Leva:

It gives me great pleasure to inform you that the Academy Board of Governors has voted to bestow a Technical Achievement Award (Academy Certificate) to **you** for the design and development of the Precision Stunt Airbag for motion picture stunt falls.

Sci/Tech Committee Chairman, Richard Edlund, will be in touch in the near future with more details, but for now please mark Saturday evening, **February 18, 2006,** on your calendar. It is then that you and a guest will be invited to attend the Scientific and Technical Awards Dinner and Ceremony at the Beverly Hilton Hotel in Beverly Hills, California. This is a black-tie event that has become a highlight affair in our Oscar season and at which your award will be presented.

Also, it affords me the opportunity of offering my congratulations in person.

Cordially,

Sid Ganis
President

SG/rm

It was from Sid Ganis, President of the Academy, congratulating me on being bestowed a Technical Achievement Award. I did it. I actually got an Academy Award.

Called my family. Reserved a table. On February 18, 2006, with my father, his wife, my mother, my wife, daughter, and my two older siblings. I attended the 2006 Scientific and Technical Achievement Awards at the Beverly Hilton hotel.

Sharing My Special Day with My Family

It was an incredible evening. News stations, magazine and trade, as well as radio stations performed interviews. The documentary crew was there too to shoot the final part of the video.

The award dinner was exciting. When I got up to the podium, I was presented with my reward by Rachel McAdams. I reminded her that we had met before. I had worked with her on "Red Eye". Besides doing stunts, I was her stunt safety. She said she was glad I was there.

It was an exciting event ending with a group shot of all the award recipients.

The Oscars!

I got amazing press for the next few weeks. "Hollywood Reporter", "Variety", "Los Angeles Times", radio and TV interviews. I was even a guest presenter at a few other non-industry award presentations. When the Oscar telecast was aired they quickly scrolled through the names of the Sci Tech Award winners. I was and still am a part of Oscar history.

The only problem was that I was not being hired. I am not sure if there was a stigma regarding the award or outright jealousy. But I was not working.

Wally Crowder (I mentioned him earlier) called me one day. Met him for lunch. He was putting out his next Stunt Players Directory and he wanted me on the cover. He said, "It's not going to make you any friends. In fact, it may piss off a few people."

I said, "You know what, you can love me or hate me, but before you open up the book, you'll have to see my face. Let's do it"."

We did it. And, yes it did not make me any friends.

6TH ANNIVERSARY EDITION

THE STUNT PLAYERS DIRECTORY

SPD 2006

BAGGING THE GOLD
Academy Award Winner
Scott Leva

Cover of the SPD

Then, my old friend I have known and worked with for many years, Don Ruffin (I mentioned him earlier in my Star Trek adventure), called me.

"You want a job?"

"You bet."

"Yeah, I figured you weren't getting many calls."

He had me work on "With Out A Trace". Nice job. Still appreciate Don. He is one of a kind and a true friend.

In 2007, I submitted again. This time for my new developments with the air ram. There was a lot of interest, and I was considered again. I demonstrated ease of take off, and multiple jumpers went one after another. All had safe take offs and landings. Fully controlled throws. It was and is unlike any other machine out there.

At this demonstration some stunt people were invited to attend and give their opinion. They basically said, no big deal. An air ram is an air ram. I did not receive the Sci Tech award. I truly believe that if stunt people were at my air bag demo, I would not have received the award then. Some of those same stuntmen have said that an air bag is an air bag. No big deal. I beg to differ.

However, in 2008, I was invited to submit my air bag to the 60th Primetime Engineering Awards, and, I did receive an award that night.

At the Emmys

In my long illustrious career, I have been nominated for a Screen Actor's Guild Award (Best Stunt Ensemble) and A Taurus Stunt Award (Best High Work and Best Overall Stunt by a Stuntman).

Nothing beats being part of Oscar history though. Nothing can take that away from me.

CHAPTER
Twenty Two

WHAT I REALLY WANT
TO DO IS DIRECT...

I loved being behind the camera more than anything. As I
mentioned earlier, I had learned from some of the best. I got the
chance to direct, mainly 2nd Unit. Being part of the Director's Guild
of America is a very proud accomplishment for me. I have been able
to create incredible action sequences as a director. This is when I am
at my most creative.

Directing 2nd Unit on "Minion"

Directing 2nd Unit on "Savage"

Directing Pick Up Shots for the Feature "Film Walking After Midnight"

As I mentioned earlier, I have been fortunate enough in my 40 + years to have worked with some of our industries greatest directors. Francis Ford Coppola ("Cotton Club"), John Huston ("Prizzi's Honor"), Steven Spielberg ("Hook"), Jud Apatow ("This Is 40") Oliver Stone ("World Trade Center"), Wes Craven ("Red Eye") Clint Eastwood (in three movies) and Mel Brookes ("Robin Hood Men In Tights,"), to name a few.

I learned something from each one.

For example, Wes Craven was low key, succinct, and to the point.

Mel Brookes kept the movie set fun and entertaining. I doubled Cary Elwes ("Robin Hood") in the scene where Robin swung in, hit one knight and the whole row toppled like dominoes. It was difficult, did multiple takes while holding my legs in an "L" position. Definitely worked my abs.

At one point I let go of the rope early, was still about eight feet off the ground, hit the floor, rolled, and did a front handspring out of it. Our stunt coordinator, Victor Paul, came over and said, I know what you did. Nice save. Victor was one of my stunt heroes. I mentioned him earlier as the original stunt double for Burt Ward on the Classic Batman series. He was also the top swordman in Hollywood at that time.

Mel Brookes came over and just loved it. "Fantastic. What is your name?"

"Scott. Scott Leva."

"Leva? That's Jewish isn't it? No. Never mind. Jews give the orders, gentiles take the orders."

I laughed. I also joked that he should have the actors sit in the banquet room with score cards like at the Olympics. He laughed, and said, "Yes". That scene with the score cards is in the movie.

Directed by Wes Craven to Look "Shocked"

With Mel Brookes and Cary Elwes

One film in particular was both a challenge, and in the end, very rewarding. Matthew Modine had written a movie called "If...Dog... Rabbit". It was released as "The Big Score". Matthew also directed and starred in it. I was hired as The Stunt Coordinator / 2nd Unit Director. Matthew did not get along with our producer. He did not like him. The problem was the producer brought me in. So, guilt by association. Matthew was not too fond of me either, originally.

I shot some decent 2nd unit scenes and worked on a few fight scenes. At one point, there was a shot where Matthew was being slammed down on a table. I suggested to the Director of

Photography (DP) that he use a certain lens. He was rather short with me and basically pushed me aside. I left him to it. I saw him check the shot afterwards. Another scene. I was looking on. Action was involved. The DP turned to me and said, "What do you think, 50mm lens?" I looked at the shot and agreed. After seeing that I was being helpful, and that the lens I suggested worked, he looked at me differently.

Matthew on the other hand. Not so much.

One night while watching dailies, my 2nd unit work was part of it. I asked Matthew to speak with me in private. I said, "Look, I know you have a problem with the producer. Do you like the work I am doing?"

"Yes..."

"Am I doing a good job?"

"Yes."

"Then don't associate me or my work with the producer, judge me on my own merit."

He looked at me differently after that. We got along better.

Every one of the crew and actors liked and respected Matthew. I did as well. I just didn't want to be an outsider.

I was able to direct Matthew in two very exciting action scenes. One was a foot chase through a cemetery. The other a motor bike / car chase through the Baja Mexico streets. I also had a 2nd Unit on the bull fighting sequence.

Directing Matthew Modine on "If...Dog...Rabbit".

In the end, it was a very positive experience. We were shooting in Baja Mexico. The main issue was the local police. They were corrupt. Being from the US side of the border, we were good targets to pull over and either pay a fine or follow them to the local police station. I was stopped once. $40.00 fine.

Now, while shooting a sequence on the beach, we had hired the local police. The chief of police was very outgoing and took a liking to me. We hired one of his police officers who turned out was the same policeman that had stopped me a few days earlier. He saw me. Got nervous. I pointed to him while talking with the police chief. He got even more nervous. All I said was how great it was to have him and his men there for the shoot.

The next day I shot a car / motorcycle chase. We used the police chief and some of his men as passengers in their own police cars while my stunt drivers did the action slides and spins.
At the end of the day, the police chief handed me his card. Said if I was ever in need of anything, contact him.

After we wrapped, payroll cut me a check. It had to be cashed at the local bank as all our funds were there. So, I cashed the checks and paid my stunt team in cash.

By then my team had returned state-side and I was on my way back as well. Stopped at the bank. Cashed the check. Had over $40,000.00 USD in my possession. As I left the bank, I made a U turn. Not illegal. But, flashing lights and siren. Oh boy. I got pulled over. I was told my U turn was illegal. Pay a fine or follow them to the local police station. The only cash I had was in the pouch with $39,960.00 more than I needed. So I said. Let's go to the station. I followed them there. As we went through the front door, the police chief was at the front desk. Amigo! Jeffe! The police men behind me went white. I had a nice chat with my friend and left. Went home and paid my stunt team. Gotta love movie making.

Another project I worked on was a featurette with a series of vignettes. Mine dealt with a young Andy Warhol. Another director on one of the vignettes was Jo Dante, so I was in good company. I was working more than one project at the time. I was also 2nd Unit Director / Stunt Coordinator on a film called "True Blue" and was rushing between sets. The Young Andy project was fun. Very creative concept. I hired my friend Scott Rhodes as the fight coordinator.

The action scenes were pretty intricate but were very well done. Especially for young actors, if I do say so myself.

On Set Directing Our Young Andy Warhol

In my opinion, Scott is one of the best fight guys in the business. Scott had worked with me on various projects in New York, as well as New Jersey. He was an asset. Scott also worked as the fight coordinator on two short films that got huge critical acclaim. "Batman Dead End" and "Worlds Finest". On "Batman Dead End", I was brought in to have the alien drop into shot, grab the Joker (Played by Andy Koenig, the son of Walter who played Chekov on the original "Star Trek"). In the same action, the alien pulled the Joker up and out of frame. I was intrigued as this had never been done before. With a series of pullies, a ratchet, and counter pressure, I achieved the goal.

Sadly a few years later, Scott had a stroke. That had pretty much taken him out of the stunt business. He started creating cool action shorts on YouTube.

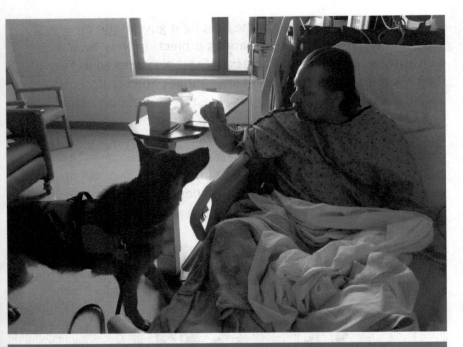

I had just finished working on a Clint Eastwood film and learned some very valuable directing tips. You are never too old to learn or too knowledgeable to add more skills to your repertoire.

About that.

I was in between jobs and training stunt people with John Moio at Bob Yerkes. High falls, air rams. John put a specific group of stuntmen together one weekend. Didn't let us know the reason.

One of the most famous, legendary stunt men in our business showed up, Buddy Van Horn. (mentioned earlier, Zorro stunt double) He was getting ready to coordinate the next Clint Eastwood film, "Flags of Our Fathers".

Buddy had been around for an eternity in the business. Doubled Guy Williams on the Disney TV series "Zorro". He had been working with Clint Eastwood for what seemed like forever. Directed three of his films.

I was literally standing in the presence of stunt royalty.

Buddy was there to find young stuntmen to play marines for the gig attack on Iwo Jima. He was looking at specific equipment. My air ram in particular.

We basically auditioned the stunt people. Buddy asked me specific questions about what my equipment could do, how was I with fire stunts? He was pleased with my answers.

Day ended. I pretty much thought I would most likely be renting equipment for this project. He was looking for younger stunt people than myself.

The next day. I get a call. "Scott?"

"Yes."

"This is Buddy Van Horn."

(Pause)

"Hello. How are you?"

"I know you are busy, but I would love to have you come on board this picture with me as my assistant stunt coordinator. While I am on first unit, you'll be handling second. While I am on second, you'll be handling first. What do you think?"

(Hell Yeah!) "That sound good. I would love to work with you."

I worked the next three weeks at Warner Brothers in the Malpasso Offices with Buddy. Met Clint. Met pretty much the whole crew. Incredible people, incredible energy.

I worked with Buddy to put a list together of potential stunt people we would bring to Iceland with us. Iceland was being used as the beaches of Iwo Jima as they most closely resembled the actual beaches. The Iwo Jima beaches were off limits as it was basically a war shrine, a memorial.

I got my equipment business partner on as one of the stunt marines. I tried to get him as many projects as possible. Sadly, not sure why, but that was never reciprocated. I think he had issues with me. Not sure. Never resolved.

We flew to Iceland.

The Stunt Crew with the Main Actors

Just the Stunt Team

We checked into our living quarters. A spa called, "The Blue Lagoon". We started to get wardrobe, props and so forth. We learned to handle the historically accurate weapons.

Our first day on set, there was a large jib arm like crane that was going to move across the hillside at the top of the beach. I had stunt people in place to fall and tumble as the crane moved past them. Two stunt people road air rams.

They did two rehearsal runs. Clint (who is known as The Boss) didn't say action or cut. He instead said, "Go and stop". Our cue for the rams would be, "Go, go!"

"Set, Go!"
The crane moved.

"Go! Go!"

The rams threw my stunt guys. Crane moved to the end.

"Stop."

I had never worked on a Clint Eastwood film and as far as I was concerned, this was going to be an all-day set up.

Then I heard, "Ok. Got it. Moving on!"

Wow. That was new and a real learning experience.

The filming was pretty much like that with quick set ups and limited takes. And you know what? It worked.

I was like a kid in a candy shop. I learned so much.

On the next day, these large Amphibious tank-like vehicles were stationed on the beach, partly in the water. I had to tie off the three stunt players who floated like dead bodies, so they would not get swept under the tanks.

I had it set. Then, I heard a voice. It's the boss. "Hey, Scott! You got everyone secured? They safe?" I looked over at Mr. Eastwood who sat atop a tank with a camera set up.

"Yes. All set." Truthfully, the only thing I could think of was, "He knows my name!"

The filming was long. Six weeks, but it seemed like so much less. I learned a lot. Had a minor incident where some of our stunt guys had a bit too much to drink. Turned over a van. Luckily no one was hurt, but I had to deal with damage control for a few days.

I tended to stay in my room at the end of the day and worked on the next day's shots for Buddy. I was not present during the van incident, but it still fell on me.

We had a few fire stunts in the movie. One dealt with two Japanese soldiers in a bunker who ran out fully engulfed in flames. I designed a specific fire mask that looked like a man screaming.

Steve Ito and Simon Rhee (my friend and co-workers from "The Return of Quan" shoot) were flown in to play Japanese soldiers and do the burn.

Simon was a little nervous. This was going to be his biggest burn. I told him that it could get claustrophobic and not to panic.

The fire stunt was set. We did a dry run rehearsal. We had fans to push the fire back.

Steve had put a mess of fire gel on his face. Way too much.

I said, it looked a bit like a porno. Clint said, "Porn is good". Always good to have a bit of levity on the set. Helped everyone relax. The fire stunt was spectacular.

Simon wore my special stunt mask, as he was doing a full burn front and back. Meanwhile Steve was set with his full back on fire, so he did not need a mask.

Definitely one for the books.

It was nominated for The World Stunt Awards for best fire stunt.

The next big burn was a marine with a flame thrower who got hit in the gas tank and blown up. I had hoped to do that one, but Buddy wanted to do it. Who am I to say no, to my boss?

We prepped it. I talked Buddy through the motions. Told him where to hit the wall, where to fall. I said once he was blown up, he would be blind. "Stay by the rock, feel the rock wall and use that to slide down," I said.

I sat next to Mr. Eastwood while Buddy got into position. "Couldn't you talk him out of it?" he asked me.

"No, could you?" I answered. He shrugged and laughed.

Go! The explosion went off. It's massive. Buddy just stood there, fully engulfed in flame. Clint and a few other people yelled, "Buddy, fall down! Fall down!" Buddy finally fell, and we put him out.

Buddy was really upset with himself. He did not follow through on the action. I told him the explosion could have easily stunned him. He felt better after that. I made sure Buddy was completely safe. He also wore one of my stunt fire masks. Even without his stumbling around and falling to the ground it was a pretty spectacular stunt.

Sadly, it was cut from the film. People that have seen the pictures are amazed by the magnitude of the explosion and fire.

Judge for yourself.

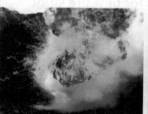  

I have two other sequences to talk about that had a lasting effect on me on this movie.

A large mountain stood in for the mountain where the famous flag raising picture was to be duplicated.

It was a long and exhausting climb. Buddy was no spring chicken. For that matter, neither was I. But Buddy had a fused ankle and was missing a lung. An old stunt injury and battle with cancer.

As we looked at this huge mountain to climb, Buddy said, "Scott go on up to the top. I'll follow after and get there when I can."

So, I climb. My stunt guys climbed. It was long. It was exhausting.

I got to the top. The shot was three Japanese soldiers shooting at our marines. They get shot. I was there and watched the set up. I was probably up there an hour already.

Clint came to me and asked what we were doing with the order of stunt Japanese soldiers getting shot and where they would be placed.

I pointed out each spot.

"Ok," he said. "You, get shot, fall, then you, and you." Then he turned to me and with a sly smile said, "So where's Buddy?"

I pointed towards the ridge we came up and as I turned to point, Buddy rose over the top of the ridge like John Wayne in "True Grit". Clint was impressed.

After we shot, I asked Clint if he could tell Buddy to ride down with him on the helicopter they used to get up there. He fully agreed.

Near the end of the shoot in Iceland we had a sequence where a medic got shot and Ryan Phillipe's character, also a medic, attempted to save him but was wounded by an explosion.

On the day Buddy said, "Scott. You'll be the marine that gets shot in the throat." I am told to go to make up to get what I am told is called the Tinsley effect prosthetic placed on my neck. It's an easily applied prosthetic that we use to hide the blood effect when I got shot. Interesting. Christian Tinsley who designed this also received a Sci Tech for his creation.

I was made up, effects put in place, suited up, and tubing went under my wardrobe to a button I would hit to shoot the blood effect from my neck. I came out.

Clint looked me over and said, "You can hide the button in your medical pouch."

Ok.

His direction. "You run, you get shot, you fall down."

"Huh? Where?"

Buddy grabbed my arm. "You start here." He pointed. Walked me over to another place. "You get shot here, you dance around, you fall here." Pointed to another place. "Got it?"

Ready to rehearse. Cameras rolled. "Right, no rehearsal. I forgot. Go!"

I ran, I got shot, I fell down.

"Don't move." Cameras came in for the next set up. This was where Ryan tried to save me before the explosion.

Interesting bit of history. I was told that the enemy would always target a medic. By taking out a medic, they could take out more soldiers that were wounded because they could not receive medical assistance.

So I laid there as the cameras were set up. Ryan talked with the medical advisor.

Clint came over. He said, "you're trying to keep him alive." Pointed to me. "You're trying to stay alive."

Ryan said, "Wait!" Then he explained all this medical stuff he would do.

Clint just shrugged. Now I'm confused. (meaning me, not Clint)

"Excuse me?" I raised my hand. Our Director of Photography, Tom Sterns said, "Yes? Oh. You want direction." A slight smirk on his face.

Clint came over. "OH. Yeah. Scott. Right." (Pause) "Don't fuck up." Looked at the crew. "Best direction I've given this whole film."

What did being an assistant stunt coordinator on a film have to do with directing, you might ask? It was an incredible learning experience. Working on an Eastwood film was like being part of a family. He was efficient, he knew what he wanted, and it was the most incredible experience I had on a film set. So much so, that I turned down bigger projects to work on two other films directed by him.

For "Letters from Iwo Jima,", we did spectacular battle sequences and another full burn that won a stunt award for best fire stunt. Again, Simon Rhee.

One night we were shooting an attack on a marine squad. Buddy was teasing me about my Academy Award. Tom Stern jumped in as well. Then, so did Clint. I said to Clint, "Hold on. What do you have? Four of these things?"

He answered, "Yes, but you don't have a People's Choice Award, do you?"

 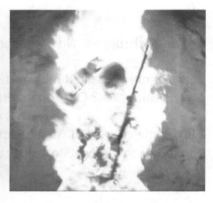

Also worked on "Changeling" starring Angelina Jolie. Buddy told me while we were working on that film that he thought it would be his last. He was tired and wanted to step down. He thought I should take over. I did not see that happening.

I got to play a Mountie in the film, who tracked down the man accused of kidnapping all these children.

There was an intricate rooftop chase that ended with a tackle and a double fall from the roof.

It was a three-day shoot. I asked Buddy to play the role of the Mountie that chased down the man suspected of kidnapping children. I had to audition for it as there was dialogue. I got into shape.

For three days I ran along the rooftop, sometimes holding a camera for point of view shots. At one-point, Clint said, "you can sit a few of the shots out if you want."

"No. I was hired for this, I can do it." And, I did.

Finished all the chase scenes and falls in the first two days, and the third day performed a rooftop jump. One of the Mounties was to miss and fall. I was supposed to barely get over, but make it.

I had a full array of air bags placed between all the jump points. For my jump, I had a harness with a wire for safety in case I couldn't grab the rail. I had safety people on the other side. Only pulled if I missed. I did not want to fall out of control to the air bag below. It was a blind fall, and difficult to judge.

We were set. I heard, "Go!" I ran, I jumped, I felt the stunt guys pull the cable full force as I took off slamming my knees first into the rail. You could hear people groan as I made contact. I was in pain. I rolled to the side of the building and looked down at cameras and the crew. I gave them a thumbs up. Then I rolled back over and laid there for a little bit as they broke for lunch. I hobbled down to my dressing room, changed, hobbled to lunch just to show that it's no big deal.

Clint asked, "Are you alright?"

I said, "I am. It comes with the territory."

My legs swelled up. It was difficult to move for a while. Had to wait for the swelling to go down before my orthopedic doctor could inject a needle and reduce the swelling by removing fluid from my knees.

The full chase was cut from the final release. I saw Mr. Eastwood at a Q & A at the Director's Guild after a screening of the film. I stopped by and said hello. He apologized for having to cut the scene. "You got hurt doing it."

I said, "No big deal. Don't apologize. It's your movie. Proud to be a part of it."

Never Before Seen Cut Footage from the "Changeling" Cut Sequence

That was the last Clint Eastwood film I worked on. Buddy said he was retiring. I would spend some time with him and his beautiful wife, Connie, at their house.

I would bring my dog, Shanti, to play. Buddy ended up getting a puppy they named Molly.

Eastwood was set to do another film, entitled, "J. Edgar" starring Leonardo DiCaprio.

I had seen the script a year before Eastwood got the rights. It was at Universal Studios then. I did not think much of it.

I was getting calls about this film. They were interviewing stunt coordinators.

A few months before, Buddy had gone in and seen Clint and told him he was done. I understand that Clint said he'd roll him out on set in a wheelchair if he had to. So, I assumed Clint did not accept Buddy's resignation.

Yet, I kept hearing about interviews for stunts for this film. I talked to Buddy. So did one of his closest friends. "The producer may think you retired. You might want to call," I said.

Buddy refused. If they wanted him, they would call.

"I understand, but they are interviewing other people for stunt coordinator."

Buddy asked, "Are you one of the people being interviewed?"

I was surprised. "Absolutely not." I would never do that without his blessing.

I found out later that a few stunt people kept putting thoughts into his ear that I was trying to push him out and take over. Far from the truth.

At one point, I decided to go to the office at Malpasso and see the producer, Rob Lorenz. I really liked Rob. A talented man, and a good director.

I went to the office without an appointment. His assistant, that I knew very well, was not too happy to see me this time. I was surprised. We always got along so well.

Rob welcomed me in. We talked small talk. He mentioned that the stunts might get cut.

I brought up Buddy. "He does not know I'm here," I said. "He would be pissed if he knew. Buddy is not retired. He is sitting home, waiting for a call. In no way, would I tell you how to do your job, or what to do in general. If you could just call Buddy. Let him know whether there are stunts or not. It would mean a lot."

He said he would.

I left. His assistant told me not to come in without an appointment in the future. She was close to Buddy as well. I am not sure if she thought I was trying to get the job or not.

A few weeks later I spoke to Buddy. They called. He was going in to get a script. Good news. "What was I doing there?" He asked.

"I just stopped in to say hello," I told him.

It seemed Rob's assistant told Buddy I came by.

I did not work on that film. It was Buddy's last one as well. Things were a little strained with us after that. I would still visit after the film wrapped. Buddy had been told by numerous sources on the film, that what he thought I did or was trying to do was way off. I don't think Buddy believed that.

During one visit, Buddy told me what he had heard before they started filming. He said Rob said I kept coming around and making a nuisance of myself.

"Rob said that?"

"Well. His assistant did."

I was only trying to help. In hindsight, I should have just left it alone.

Our relationship was the never the same. I saw Buddy at a funeral for another stuntman. We spoke. I asked about his grandchildren. He was pleasantly surprised I remembered them. Of course, I knew them well. During our friendship, his granddaughter and my daughter were friends. I got them into Disneyland through my connections. I remembered them well. Buddy actually seemed happy to see me.

Sadly, Buddy passed away in 2021. I wish we had cleared the air. I never got around to it.

Our business can be tough. It can be competitive. Sometimes it is hard to have real friends in the stunt world. Especially if you are competing for the same job. I have lost a few friends over misunderstandings and pettiness. It comes with the territory. It is sad when you think that, oftentimes, your life is in the hands of some of your "friends".

CHAPTER
Twenty Three

SPIDER-MAN NO MORE

During this time, Spider-Man became less and less a part of my life. Especially after the whole "will he - won't he" Spider-Man movie ordeal. I backed off a bit. I sold my entire bound collection of Marvel and non-Marvel books to Bill at the Golden Apple.

I slowly started to move away from Spider-Man.

However, before completely abandoning that part of my life, I did an Exercise Video "Spider-Man Super Fit: Youth Fitness System" as Spidey and Peter Parker. It was awful.

Jumping into Action for Spidey Super Fit

I had a few special Marvel / Spider-Man events left in me.

Danny Fingeroth contacted me. He was going to do two Holodisk Spider-Man covers. The Holodisk is a 3D disk that by shining a pin light and turning it around, it moves.

There were two different versions: Peter Parker / Spider-Man and The Scarlett Spider. Danny always made these fun. It was one of the most memorable times I had doing a cover.

The best way to see the way cool Peter/Spidey holodisk on the cover (if you have the enhanced version of this mag) is to hold a penlight or other direct light over the disk and slowly turn the comic around. You'll see Spidey moving and Pete snapping a photo and flashing a smile. Looks pretty neat in sunlight, too.

By the way, the credits for this disk and the one on WEB #125 are:
Spidey/Scarlet and Spider/Peter: SCOTT LEVA
Set Design: CRAIG NEWSWANGER and RYDER for CFC Applied Holographics and Polaroid.
Holography: CRAIG NEWSWANGER and RYDER for CFC Applied Holographics and Polaroid
Directed by: DANNY FINGEROTH

The Covers for The Holodisk Books

Best Pictures I Could Get Showing the Disks

First and Only "Live" Appearance of The Scarlet Spider

That was my last official job with Marvel Comics.

Not my last for Marvel Promotions.

For one event, they wanted the superheroes to parachute down onto fairgrounds. I did not suit up for that event. I got professional stunt man and a skydiver, Ted Barba, to wrangle that one for me. I coordinated on the ground.

Cool to see the colorful Marvel heroes float down on parachutes.

Another dealt with National Comic Book Day. They had the Macy's Spider-Man balloon there. I was asked to be Johnny Storm, The Human Torch. The fiery member of the Fantastic Four along with Sue Storm who was the Invisible Woman and Reed Richards who was Mr. Fantastic. Not sure if The Thing was there. I even had to wear a cheap blonde wig.

Was contacted about doing another charity event for Henry Winkler and his wife, Stacey. They were involved in various children's charities. They had a who's who of A list celebrities including Mel Gibson, Anthony Perkins, and Paul Reubens (Pee Wee Herman) to name a few. There were a huge number of celebrities, I think Henry Winkler called in a lot of favors. I only met Mel Gibson before I suited up, so everyone else saw me as Spider-Man.

Mr. Gibson and Me. I Am Wearing the Cannon Spidey Jacket

Some of the most fun I had was hanging out with Paul Reubens. I must admit, I was not a fan of Pee Wee Herman. I knew the show, but never watched it until after we met and became friends.

After the event, I gave Paul my information. He wanted to stay in touch.

A few days later Paul called me and asked me to dress up as Spider-Man for a surprise birthday Party for Cassandra Peterson (Elvira).

I was happy to oblige. Some people were there that you would recognize, I forget who. Elvira was running late. It was a surprise party, so how would she know? We thought she had arrived. The lights were turned off. I waited with everyone in pitch black darkness, for what seemed like forever.

"Great," I said. "A strange man asks me to dress up in tights and hang out in a house with strangers in the dark. This isn't creepy."

Paul said, "No! It's not like that."

Obviously, I was just kidding. The first time they turned the lights out, it was a false alarm, no Elvira. The second time was great, the surprise was a hit.

I would visit Paul's home near Bronson Canyon and was one of his guest for the preview opening of The Star Tours Ride at Disney Land. Paul was the voice of the droid pilot. I even had a small part as a postal worker delivering the box with Grace Jones in it for his holiday special show. He was the type of friend that I could text out of the blue and we would pick up right where we left off. And, on my birthday, he constantly sent texts with videos and images. He really made me feel special. We drifted apart after a while, but Paul got in touch with me again a few years ago. I am glad he did.

When Paul passed away, it left a hole in my heart. He had that effect on just about everyone he knew. I will miss him forever.

My truly last official appearance for Marvel was for the Rose Parade in a Spider-Man action event before the day of the parade. I was

Marvel Promotions only resident stuntman. I asked for an exorbitant amount of money. They agreed. I hired stunt people to play the roles. My partner with our equipment played the Green Goblin. Stuntwoman Caryn was Spider-woman. I, of course, was Spider-Man. We had mats, airbags, mini trampolines. The works. We rehearsed. I had written the script.

With a few of the stunt people, we did an audio recording. I did both Spidey and the Goblin. Caryn voiced Spider-Woman.

It was a lot of fun. After the show we met the crowd. Usual appearance stuff.

As I mentioned early on, as part of my tools I used 1/6 scale action figures to demonstrate the more complex rigging and wire stunts. Through the years I have acquired quite the collection.
My wife suggested I set up a display case for them. I think she regrets that now. One of my prized pieces is a 1/6 scale Spider-Man / Peter Parker that a very talented friend made for me which is similar to the photo cover I did many years ago.

Later on, I dressed up for some nephews. Family stuff. Another one of my nephews was Spider-Man for Halloween in my honor. His mother made a brilliant costume.

Do I miss it? No. A part of Spidey is still in me. Always will be. I had exciting times. Was a part of the Marvel Universe. Who could ask for anything better than that?

CHAPTER
Twenty Four

LIFE IS WHAT HAPPENS TO YOU WHILE YOU'RE BUSY MAKING OTHER PLANS

So, what now? Life has its ups and downs. I am still involved in the Industry. The industry has changed. I no longer get blown up or thrown through windows. I tell other people to do that now.

My wife and daughter are both working more in the industry. Early on, my wife played a role in a film in which I was a stunt coordinator. She had to do stunts, too. She was ratcheted back onto a table after being shot by Ernie Hudson of "Ghostbuster" fame.

Scott Rhodes, My Wife and My Equipment Partner on Set

My daughter has been booking acting roles pretty steadily for a while. Things were good.

I became more involved with family, mainly, my mother. It had been difficult.

My mother and father divorced way back when I was living in New York. My father remarried. A lovely woman. Susan. They are the perfect couple.

My mother met a man, Paul. They moved to New Mexico. They never married, but they were together for over 20 years. He passed away in 2019. I came out to help her. It became a very difficult situation. My mother was looking for another Paul. She would occasionally call me Paul by mistake. She wanted another companion. Someone to talk to, sit with her while she did her crossword puzzles, watched TV at an extremely high volume. I stopped being her son. I was a caregiver, a housekeeper, a cook, and a nurse. My work suffered and my home life suffered. My wife and daughter were in Los Angeles. I was in Albuquerque.

I had my dog, a beautiful German Shepherd, Zascha. She was also my service dog. I was severely injured many years back on a TV series. Car hit stunt. I bounced off the hood and hit the windshield. I suffered severe brain trauma. And with extreme stress, I can have black outs. Zascha was my savior. She was trained as a seizure alert dog.

I was losing business back home. The Covid pandemic hit. It was impossible to go anywhere.

When the pandemic subsided a bit, I was set to head home to take care of business. If I did not do this, I would lose thousands of dollars that I could not afford to lose.

Before the pandemic, if I went back to Los Angeles, my mother would come with me. She refused to fly. So, we drove. Thirteen hours.

Problem was she just wanted to sit around and watch TV and do her crossword puzzles. My mother had bad knees. I did too.

She was having difficulty walking. I had set up some visits with some doctors while she was in California. She went to a few appointments then wanted to go home. She would cry non-stop. I finally gave in and took her back home.

The pandemic finally settled down a bit, and this made it easier to travel finally. I rented a car. This time my mother stayed home. It was too difficult for her to travel. I had a caregiver that was there to help, besides I would only be gone a few weeks.

Then the Pandemic hit its second wave. New Mexico closed its borders to travel, our caregivers husband got Covid. She would quarantine for the at least 10 days. My mother would be mostly alone.

I had decided to finally have knee replacement surgery as there was nothing else to do. So this limited my travelling.

My mother got angry when she got older. She would ostracize just about everyone in the family. My middle brother, my older brother who transitioned and is now my sister. (I fully support her decision.) Even my wife. This made it difficult to get the family to help.

So, with the help of Paul's daughter (I just realized, there were a lot of Pauls in my life) we got my older sister to come out, much to my mother's protest. I told her, she needed someone there and my sister could help.

There is way more to this story, but I am summarizing and choosing to leave out some of the more uncomfortable parts.

My sister arrived and after close to three months with our mother she decided it was best to get her to Texas to be closer to her and my other brother. My mother agreed but was not happy. There was a lot of strain on our family. There still is.

My mother passed away November of 2022.

It hurts, but it's a different kind of hurt. My sister also went through no longer being her child. Just a caregiver, a housekeeper, a cook, and a nurse.

Maybe one day we can all put everything behind us and become a family again.

In the meanwhile, the Pandemic took its toll on everyone. Financially, things were a disaster.

Once we started getting back on track our Unions went on strike. Again, financially another disaster.

My pup Zascha passed away. Devastating. If you have a family pet, you'll understand the loss.

So, what do you do?

Me? I wrote this book that I have been planning to do for the past 25 or so years. I am looking into developing an exciting TV series that I am sure will be a hit. If I told you what it was about you would probably agree. I say this, as I have been involved in the industry for over 40 plus years. I have developed a pretty good idea on what might or might not work.

Many years ago, I approached a friend of mine who was a producer for one of the big studios that had successful movies and TV shows. I gave him about six months of comics of a new book that had just come out. I explained that was about the characters. It needed to be on cable, not a network.

A few weeks later he told me that he didn't think it would do that well. That idea was the "Walking Dead". A year later Frank Darabont found the comic book series, and the rest is history.

I also pitched the idea of a British TV series I was watching. It was about a woman who inherited her old family's mansion, and with her husband wanted to make it into a hotel. It was inhabited by a ghost that had passed away there. She has an accident that caused her to see and talk with the ghost. Again. I was told not a good idea. Someone thought it would work and "Ghost" is now one of the top shows here on CBS.

I have not always been right. I didn't think "Hannah Montana" would last after I worked on it in the beginning. My daughter told me otherwise. Also, I did not feel that "The Boys" would translate well onto the screen. Too sexual. Too violent. They did a hell of a job. Pretty much adapted it the way it was written. It worked. That being said, I will be pitching my ideas in the near future.

I also will be working on my short film, "Bloom in Spring". Finished the script at least.

I hope to make amends and rekindle relationships that have gone sour. There are friends that have helped me in the industry in the past. One who was probably the biggest stunt coordinator in our industry at one time. He gave me some of the biggest stunts in my career and some of the biggest opportunities as well. I miss him. I hope we can fix things.

So like Spider-Man trapped under that tonnage of wreckage back in Spider-Man # 33. I won't give up. I will persevere.

Is this the end of my story?

Life is filled with possibilities and new challenges. I look to a new beginning.

My Father and His Wife Susan

My Mother and Paul

My Dog and Me

Me, Zascha, My Daughter and My Wife in 2010. Still Going Strong

Running Wild Press publishes stories that cross genres with great stories and writing. RIZE publishes great genre stories written by people of color and by authors who identify with other marginalized groups. Our team consists of:

Lisa Diane Kastner, Founder and Executive Editor
Joelle Mitchell, Licensing and Strategy Lead
Cody Sisco, Acquisitions Editor, RIZE
Benjamin White, Acquisition Editor, Running Wild
Peter A. Wright, Acquisition Editor, Running Wild
Resa Alboher, Editor
Rebecca Dimyan, Editor
Andrew DiPrinzio, Editor
Abigail Efird, Editor
Rod Gilley, Editor
Aimee Hardy, Editor
Henry L. Herz, Editor
Laura Huie, Editor
Cecilia Kennedy, Editor
Barbara Lockwood, Editor
Evangeline Estropia, Product Manager
Pulp Art Studios, Cover Design
Standout Books, Interior Design
Polgarus Studios, Interior Design

Learn more about us and our stories at www.runningwildpublishing.com

Loved this story and want more? Follow us at www.runningwildpublishing.com, www.facebook/runningwildpress, on Twitter @lisadkastner @RunWildBooks, on YouTube at https://www.youtube.com/channel/UCDZsgnRW_PakI0LSvMXN5og on LinkedIn at https://www.linkedin.com/company/runningwildpress/ https://www.linkedin.com/company/rwp-rize/